Writers of Italy Series

General Editor
C.P. Brand
Professor of Italian
University of
Edinburgh

6

LEOPARDI

© G. Carsaniga 1977
Edinburgh University Press
22 George Square, Edinburgh

ISBN 0 85224 297 2

Printed in Great Britain by
W.& J.Mackay Limited
Chatham

*

Edinburgh University Press

Giacomo

LEOPARDI

The unheeded voice

GIOVANNI CARSANIGA

*

Contents

Preface

This is only the nucleus of a much larger 'book' that the reader should ideally build up in his own mind by studying all Leopardi's writings, in particular all the pages of the *Zibaldone* referred to in the text, and checking my opinions and his own against those of the critics mentioned in the notes to each chapter, and in the bibliographies attached to their works. Although I did my best to include in this book all the points that seemed important to me, and are traditionally considered important in Leopardian criticism, I cannot claim completeness nor do I wish to. This is especially true of my comments on the *Canti*. I have tried to give examples of possible approaches, examining some poems from a stylistic angle, describing the lexical and semantic connections between some others, analyzing images sometimes from the point of view of their historical development and sometimes for their psychological relevance, identifying possible sources in Italian and foreign literature, not to mention, of course, Leopardi's own prose works. It is clear that if I had to apply all these, and many other possible methods (for instance, the study of Leopardi's corrections) to each and every poem, I should have had to write a book at least twice as long, and possibly half as useful. It is up to the reader to apply to a given text the insights he may have derived from our joint examination of the others. The notes refer only to a small number of the works I have consulted, and found useful to develop my argument. They should be taken as suggestions for further reading and not as a general bibliography.

In my opinion Leopardi was not only a great poet but the greatest Italian thinker of his age, though his philosophy did not and could not have the impact of the thought of Cattaneo, Cavour and De Sanctis, whom Gaetano Salvemini in 1949 mentioned together with Leopardi as 'the only four (Italian) men of genius of the nineteenth century' ('Manzoni, Mazzini and Carducci', he added, 'I would put among the second-rate men'). I have therefore given great importance to the development of his philosophical speculation, not only in connection with his poetic works but also in the absolute. A great deal of work still remains to be done on Leopardi's scientific culture, and the importance of his friendship and contacts with scientists like Puccinotti, Tommasini, Paoli and others often mentioned in his letters and in the *Zibaldone*: I hope soon to publish a study specifically devoted to this problem.

This book is 'objective' only in the scientific sense that my statements are objectively verifiable and open to discussion, but not in the sense that I have tried to keep at equal distance from all possible critical, philosophical and political opinions. In fact it will be clear from the book that I sympathize with most of Leopardi's views, many of which I find applicable to the ideological configuration of to-day's world, and to the cultural situation of contemporary Italy. I believe the best way of stimulating others freely to draw their own conclusions is to give up any pretence of impartiality and declare openly my own bias.

I am greatly in debt, for the development of my interest in Leopardi, to Cesare Luporini, Walter Binni and Sebastiano Timpanaro, with whom I came into contact during my student days at the Scuola Normale Superiore in Pisa, and to John Humphreys Whitfield who patiently presided over my novitiate as a university teacher. Their books have been a constant source of inspiration to me. I am thankful to my friends Peter Brand, Lino Pertile and Riccardo Steiner for their perceptive comments and helpful suggestions on many aspects of this book; and to Umberto Bosco, Direttore del Centro Nazionale di Studi Leopardiani, for giving me a grant to attend the III Convegno Internazionale di Studi Leopardiani in 1972. I am also grateful to the University of Western Australia for subsidizing my travel to read a paper on 'Leopardi e la scienza' at the ninth Conference of the Associazione Internazionale per gli studi di lingua e letteratura italiana, and enabling me to tidy up certain aspects of my research in the libraries of Pisa and Florence; and for providing a most congenial atmosphere in which to finish the book. Mrs Nancy Woodward, secretary to the Italian Department, was responsible for the dramatic improvement in the standard of typing, which she took over from me after the first seven chapters.

All references are to *Tutte le opere*, edited by W. Binni and Enrico Ghidetti (Florence 1969). In the case of the *Zibaldone* (volume II of this edition) Leopardi's original page number is given. All other references are from volume I, in which case the roman numeral I precedes the page number; the figure 1 or 2 after the page number indicates that the quotation is from the left or right-hand column.

All the English translations, which I have tried to keep more faithful to the meaning than to the form of the originals, and in no way to attempt to reproduce their literary qualities, are mine.

G. C., *Western Australia, July 1976*

1. 'Dearest Father...'

'Dearest Father', Giacomo wrote in Latin at the age of nine to Count Monaldo Leopardi, on 16 October 1807:

> We resumed our studies with great joy four days ago. I hope they will proceed according to your, and our tutor's, wishes. I will attend to them with all my heart; and study will be more pleasant to me than play. I also desire, on the other hand, to relax my spirit from time to time, and you must be prepared to be forbearing. I hope you will be, because I know how much you love me; and I want to be able to correspond, as I must, to the benevolence you show me. This I will do with God's help.

Monaldo was then thirty-one. His wife, Marchesa Adelaide Antici, was two years younger. Giacomo, the first of their ten sons (of whom only five survived birth or infancy), was born almost exactly nine months after the marriage. Of his parents, Monaldo was the one with whom Giacomo was able to have some sort of communication. Adelaide was a hard, unfeeling woman, who, while performing her duties of housewife, and administrator of the distressed Leopardi estate, strode about the house in a pair of men's riding boots, with the hem of her black skirt tucked into her waist, and a sailor's hat on her head. She never hugged or kissed her children: a look was her only caress. Her daughter Paolina defined her in a letter as

> an ultra-bigoted person, a real surfeit of Christian perfection, who puts an unimaginable amount of strictness in all details of domestic life. A truly good and exemplary woman, she set herself totally impracticable standards of austerity, and imposed upon herself duties towards her children which are quite inconvenient for them.

What Giacomo himself thought of his mother is revealed in three terrifying pages of the *Zibaldone* (353–6). All his filial affection was therefore channelled towards his father, of whom more was perhaps expected than he was able to give.

Monaldo was a staunch Catholic, but not so bigoted as his wife. He was not impressed by images of the Madonna rolling their eyes

in times of political tension. His forthrightness and outspokenness
had made him several enemies in the Papal court, and he was not
afraid of criticizing the Pope himself. No doubt his strength of
character and his intellectual and ideological consistency set a
valuable standard for Giacomo. He was one of those conservatives
who believed that the world was being swept by a wave of per-
verted and destructive liberalism, and was convinced that a conservative should swim against the tide, as he was prepared to do. He was
therefore often critical of established authority and occasionally open
to new ideas (he was probably the first father in the States of the
Church to have his sons vaccinated against smallpox). When he was
young he was sharply critical of his own parents' practice of keeping
him without money, and of the old-fashioned and unimaginative
teaching methods of his tutor Don Giuseppe Torres. Once a parent
himself, he gave Giacomo money—even if not as much or as
regularly as his son needed; he also replaced Torres, who had stayed
on in the household, with Don Sebastiano Sanchini (the teacher
mentioned in Giacomo's 1807 letter). By 1812 Giacomo had been
taught all Don Sebastiano knew—which was not much—and
Monaldo sought the friendship of a much better scholar, Johann
Caspar Vogel, an Alsatian refugee who lived in Recanati between
1806 and 1814 and became canon of Recanati Cathedral in 1809.
Giacomo benefited considerably from this relationship. Vogel and
Monaldo frequently exchanged books; and it was this priest who
probably gave Giacomo the idea of keeping a sort of diary-cum-
notebook and calling it *Zibaldone*. Monaldo fostered in Giacomo an
abiding love for study in general, and literature and philosophy in
particular. With whatever slender means he could wheedle out of
Adelaide, who sternly held the purse strings, he bought books for
his library, which by the time Giacomo was finally allowed the first
taste of independence (a journey to Rome in 1822) numbered about
12,000 volumes. It was a wise and farsighted cultural investment,
more than any of Monaldo's wealthier contemporaries had ever
done for their children: probably no other Italian writer had such
good educational opportunities as Giacomo Leopardi. He also had
the invaluable advantage of being in a position to perceive very
clearly and from an early age the limitations of his own education
and upbringing: not only because of his unusual intelligence, but
also because Monaldo, though a narrow-minded reactionary who
would have liked his son to share his views, was no brainwasher, and
preferred persuasion to compulsion.

In 1810 the twelve-year old Giacomo composed and wrote out in his extremely neat and tidy handwriting (which Professor Corti finds it difficult not to construe as a symptom of psychological repression), a verse fable, *L'Ucello*. Its source was a cautionary tale by the Jesuit Giovan Battista Roberti (1719–86) about the dangers of freedom: the story of a bird that escaped one day from its secure cage where it enjoyed its mistress's love and perished in a bird-catcher's net. The child poet completely reversed the moral of the story: though the bird has all it needs in its gilded cage, it feels happier outside it. 'The love of freedom reigns in a young heart.' The word 'cage' again appears to denote his home town and 'accursed house' in a letter Giacomo wrote to Pietro Giordani nine years later (I, 1079, 2), at a time of crisis, when he found his need to escape from Recanati, to travel and nourish his mind with fresh intellectual stimuli, repeatedly frustrated by Monaldo's uncompromising and seemingly obtuse opposition. The clash between father and son was long and bitter and left deep scars.

In its ambiguity, shown by its two contrasting interpretations, the caged bird story is an appropriate symbol of Giacomo's reactions to his family life. His home, the gilded cage, was the prison he wanted to escape from, but also the place he felt most secure in and longed to go back to when he was away from it, as appears from his letters (I, 1130, 2; 1213, 1), and from the *Zibaldone* (4226–7). Monaldo had realized quite early, when the boy was only fifteen, the incompleteness of an exclusively home-based education and the need to let him travel and broaden his mind. The father's opinion of Recanati was no better than the son's: it was 'a prison', a 'dark cavern' where 'meanness and stupidity are esteemed and praised more than intelligence, merit and virtue'. Monaldo thought that 'he who feels himself a cut above the rest should flee his home town': for him, however, the head of Recanati's first family, there was no escape. Given Adelaide's character, as different from his 'as the sky is different from the earth', family life held no great attractions for him. Giacomo was the only friend he had or could hope to have in Recanati, and he could not bear the idea of letting his son leave the family.

Much has been written on the relationship between Giacomo and his father, especially in the second half of the last century. One finds two main contrasting opinions: that Monaldo was a good and loving father who did all that was in his power to help and support a difficult and often ungrateful son; and, on the other hand, that he was a selfish and narrow-minded autocrat who, because of his rigid and blinkered views, would not give young Giacomo the freedom and independence he needed. Critics have passionately argued in favour of either view as if a better understanding of Giacomo's poetry depended upon one or the other being accepted as true. It was a pointless argument—firstly on psychological grounds. Since Monaldo's make-up, like everyone else's, contained a mixture of contrasting feelings and motivations, *both* views are true. His love for Giacomo was deep and genuine insofar as it arose out of a genuine emotional dependence on him: precisely for this reason, however, he hated to see his son becoming independent. Giacomo's own emotional response was equally ambivalent, and there is no need to accuse him of hypocrisy over the discrepancy between his affectionate letters to his father and the bitterness with which he referred to him in his letters to his brother Carlo and his friend Giordani. Like many reactionary thinkers Monaldo was extremely sensitive to political wrongdoings and moral evil, and in his denunciation of them he was often right; but his diagnosis of their causes and the remedies he proposed were mostly short-sighted and wrong. Father and son each disliked what the other thought and stood for, but they had affection and respect for each other at least as profound and lasting as the differences that divided them.

The debate whether Giacomo was great because of, or in spite of, Monaldo is critically pointless on methodological grounds also. The use of biographical data and psychological inferences to throw light on a poet's work is all too often part of a circular argument in which the poet's work has itself been used as a major source of psychological inferences and biographical data. Now circular arguments are not in themselves invalid. A great deal can be learned from a circular investigation process in which data of various kinds are established and related to each other. The wider the circle, the better. All sectors of the circle can be chosen as targets for different investigations, but no sector can be at the same time the object and the datum of any single investigation. Furthermore, the relationship between the datum and the object cannot be assumed *a priori* to be one of cause and effect, because the very nature of the relationship is part of the problem. To think otherwise would be to use a slightly less crude version of the critical method rejected by Leopardi himself in his letter to Louis De Sinner of 24 May 1832 (1, 1382, 2), against those who saw a causal link between his physical illnesses and disabilities and his *philosophie désespérante*.

Voi dite benissimo ch'egli è assurdo l'attribuire ai miei scritti
una tendenza religiosa. Quels que soient mes malheurs, qu'on a
jugé à propos d'étaler et que peut-être on a un peu éxagérés...
j'ai eu assez de courage pour ne pas chercher à en diminuer le
poids ni par de frivoles espérances d'une prétendue félicité
future et inconnue, ni par une lâche resignation. Mes sentimens
envers la destinée ont été et sont toujours ceux que j'ai exprimés
dans *Bruto minore*. Ç'a été par suite de ce même courage,
qu'étant amené par mes recherches à une philosophie désespérante, je n'ai pas hésité à l'embrasser toute entière; tandis que de
l'autre côté ce n'a été que par effet de la lâcheté des hommes, qui
ont besoin d'être persuadés du merite de l'existence, que l'on a
voulu considérer mes opinions philosophiques comme le
résultat de mes souffrances particulières, et que l'on s'obstine
d'attribuer à mes circonstances matérielles ce qu'on ne doit
qu'à mon entendement. Avant de mourir, je vais protester
contre cette invention de la faiblesse et de la vulgarité, et prier
mes lecteurs de s'attacher à détruire mes observations et mes
raisonnemens plutôt que d'accuser mes maladies. [You are
absolutely right in saying that it is absurd to attribute to my
writings a religious tendency. Whatever my misfortunes, which
it was thought appropriate to disclose and perhaps to exag-
gerate somewhat, I have had enough courage not to attempt to
lessen their weight, either through frivolous hopes in an alleged
future and unknown happiness, or through a cowardly resignation. My feelings towards destiny have been and are still those I
expressed in *Bruto minore*. It was because of that same courage
that, having been led by my researches towards a philosophy of
hopelessness, I have had no hesitation in embracing it in its
entirety; whereas, on the other hand, it was because of the
cowardice of men, who need to be persuaded that their
existence has merit, that my philosophical opinions have been
taken as the consequence of my individual sufferings, and what
is due only to my understanding of things has been attributed
to my material circumstances. Before I die I am going to
protest against such fabrications which arise out of feebleness
and vulgarity, and beg my readers to apply themselves to
destroying my observations and arguments, rather than impute
them to my infirmities.]
It is significant that this passage was written by Leopardi in French,
within an Italian letter, as if he had wanted to make himself perfectly

clear to De Sinner, with no possibility of misunderstanding. Of course there *was* a link between Leopardi's infirmities (a deformation of his spine, and many other gastro-intestinal complaints mostly of psychosomatic origin, but no less serious or disabling for all that) and his philosophy of despair; for all events in a man's life are interrelated. This should be a point not worth discussing, but a basic assumption. But was it a *causal* link? Many a philosopher of despair enjoyed good health and a perfectly straight spine. I can think of at least one hunchback who was a forward-looking optimistic Christian. Once we take the link for granted we can perceive the real question, which is: *how* did Leopardi's physical suffering relate to his world view? *how* did he sublimate his disabilities and pains into a remarkably rich creative activity? Long before psychoanalysis became fashionable (Freud was still practising hypnosis at this time) Alphonse Daudet attributed the source of Leopardi's misery to his 'enfance sans tendresse'; and the reason for the bitterness pervading his work and the blackness of despair generating his verse to the fact that he lacked 'la caresse chaude, la Mama'. That may well be true, given what is known of Giacomo's mother. But it is irrelevant in order to appreciate the particular set of symbols Leopardi chose to express his state of mind, and the constructive use to which he put the emptiness of his childhood. He could have written sentimental verse about *mamma*, or *mamma*-like women, or Woman seen as the embodiment of Motherhood, like scores of minor Italian versifiers; or he could have evolved a poetic theory in which the poet is seen as the eternal child, as Pascoli did. Instead he developed an extremely coherent and significant symbolization of the human condition in its ambivalent relationship to nature, both parent and oppressor; and of man's continual search for personal identity, both as an individual and as a social being. He made a 'poetic' use of his symbols, 'poetic', that is, in its etymological meaning of 'constructive'. Poetry was largely irrelevant to human life in early nineteenth-century Italy (perhaps it still is). Leopardi began to make it relevant to all he read, thought, felt and did. He then showed how poetry (not only *his* poetry) could become relevant to all—to all of us, to-day.

He wanted to talk to us: one of the literary projects that occupied his mind, at least from 1821 to 1827, was a *Letter to a young man of the twentieth century* (1, 371, 1; *Zib.* 4280). To-day it is fashionable to say, speaking of writers who sell an idea for a TV serial, that they have 'created' the theme. Let us leave the use of this verb to them. Leopardi did not create anything. He laboriously constructed his world-view, his art, his work, out of existing materials. As a lifelong classicist, he avoided the pitfalls of 'originality' in the Romantic sense. Most of his ideas are demonstrably derivative and unoriginal, deeply rooted in a well-attested philosophical tradition. But tradition was for him a starting point, not a goal, as for many classicists of his age. For him originality was 'an acquired faculty, like all others' (*Zib.* 2186; see also 1698, 2228–9); it was—according to the well-known classical simile of the honey-bee—a distillation of many diverse cultural juices preserved into a systematically organized intellectual honeycomb. What strikes one about his 'system' is not that it was logically consistent or philosophically watertight; it is the way he turned imbalance and contradiction into the sharpest of intellectual tools. It has long been debated whether Leopardi was, or was not, a philosopher. The answer may be that he did not take philosophy as an end but as a means of understanding reality, particularly his own contemporary reality, in all its aspects, from religion to technology, from linguistics to sociology, from politics to poetry—and as a means of changing it. Many critics have blamed Leopardi for his allegedly negative attitude to change. Of course, he could not change the direction of scientific and technological progress, the lines of development of the industrial revolution, the shape of Italian society. He was only a poet: and he changed poetry.

2. 'Peregrine and Recondite Erudition'

Giacomo's schooling, like his father's before him, was based on learning by heart a vast amount of prescribed notions, presented in such a way as to make them appear related not to the facts of life but to some mysterious and incomprehensible power ritual. What these notions were and how they were organized can be gathered from the syllabuses of three of the annual examinations that Giacomo, his brother Carlo and his sister Paolina sat publicly at their home in the presence of teachers, relatives and friends from 1808 to 1812. They were based on some of the best known textbooks of that time. Although Giacomo never explicitly condemned his own schooling, the unfavourable opinion he had of the educational methods he experienced is clear from several pages of the *Zibaldone* (45, 1063–4, 1472–3, 3839). And yet, in one vital respect, his education was profoundly different from that of most of his contemporaries. There was in it an element of freedom. Monaldo had provided two escape routes. First, he let Giacomo use the family library at will (as soon as the boy was fifteen a religious dispensation was obtained allowing him to read forbidden books). Then, he encouraged him to do what Giacomo had called, in his 1807 letter, 'animum relaxare' that is, write poetry, read literature, and learn freely on his own. In 1808 Giacomo had already begun to educate himself independently of his tutors. The following year he began to take so much advantage of his freedom to do what he wanted within the confines of the family library (the *only* freedom he had) that by 1817 he had permanently ruined his health.

The amount of work he did in those years was prodigious. His translations from Latin, Latin compositions, Italian prose and verse writings in 1809 and 1810 fill a 500-page volume in Professor Maria Corti's critical edition. In 1811 he translated Horace's *Ars Poetica* in *ottava rima*, wrote a tragedy in three acts, *La virtú indiana* [Indian Virtue], and a philosophical dissertation *Sopra l'anima delle bestie* [Whether Animals Have A Soul]. In 1812 he wrote another tragedy, *Pompeo in Egitto* [Pompey in Egypt], some epigrams, and a philosophical dialogue *Sopra un moderno libro intitolato 'Analisi delle idee ad uso della gioventù*' [On a Modern Book Entitled 'Analysis of Ideas for the Use of Young People'], and began to write a scientific treatise *Storia dell'Astronomia* [History of Astronomy] which he finished the following year. His formal education being completed, Giacomo began to study Greek and Hebrew by himself, and, at the end of August 1814, presented his father with a 352-page manuscript containing an edition and a commentary of Porphyry's *Life of Plotinus* which, in spite of its obvious shortcomings, due to the fact that Giacomo could not examine the principal codices, was praised by the Swedish scholar Johann David Akerblad. Other extremely learned philological works followed suit. In 1815 he composed in two months the interesting *Saggio sopra gli errori popolari degli antichi* [Essay on the Popular Errors of the Ancients]; and took six months to write another commentary on the works of Julius Africanus. Between May and June he composed the *Orazione agli Italiani in occasione della liberazione del Piceno* [Oration to the Italians on the Occasion of the Liberation of Piceno], inspired by the defeat of Murat's army at Tolentino on 2 May. In the summer he translated Moschus's Idylls and the *Batrachomyomachia*. From January to April 1816 he translated among other things the works of the Latin rhetor Marcus Cornelius Fronto that had recently been discovered by Angelo Mai, and wrote a dissertation on his life and works; he also published *Notizie istoriche e geografiche sulla città e chiesa arcivescovile di Damiata* [Historical and Geographical Facts about the Town and Cathedral of Damietta], a learned review of an Italian verse translation (based on an Italian prose translation) of the Hebrew Psalter, a dissertation *Della fama di Orazio presso gli antichi* [On Horace's Fame Among the Ancients], and excerpts from his own translations from Homer's *Odyssey*. In May and July he sent to the influential Milanese review *Biblioteca Italiana* two letter-articles concerning the question of translations. The second was a reply to Madame De Staël's famous essay, *De l'esprit des traductions*, which started one of the most protracted and fierce controversies between Classicists and Romantics in Italy. Neither was published. He did not neglect poetry. In the Spring he wrote *Inno a Nettuno* [Hymn to Neptune] purporting to be a translation from the Greek, and *Le rimembranze* [Remembrances]; and in the late Autumn *Appressamento della morte* [The Approach of Death]: the last two rather funereal in inspiration and mood. He made further translations the following year: Aesiod's *Battle of Titans*, and the fragments by Dionysius of Halicarnassus, discovered by Mai; another article for

Lo Spettatore on points of lexicography; he also wrote poetry, including his first love-poem inspired by a visit in December of his married cousin Gertrude Cassi-Lazzeri. In 1817 he also started his correspondence with Pietro Giordani, and began keeping a diary. He was by then in a very poor state of health. In his third letter to Giordani (1, 1023–8) he wrote: 'My physical condition is not merely weak but extremely weak, and I will not deny that it was somewhat affected by my exertions in the past six years'. About a year later (1, 1050) he explicitly declared to Giordani: 'I ruined myself during seven years of mad and desperate study, at the very time I was growing up and my body needed to become stronger'.

I have set out in detail the catalogue of Leopardi's indefatigable activity between 1811 and 1817 because he himself singled out those years as critical. They were decisive not only for his physical health but also for his intellectual formation. In that period he relentlessly explored and absorbed the most varied cultural material. He learned a number of languages: Latin, Greek, Hebrew, Spanish (probably with the help of Francisco Serrano, the Spanish rector of the local seminary who taught him to draw). Through language learning and translating he acquired a lasting interest in theoretical linguistic problems: not only in the field of classical philology, in which he was one of the most accomplished scholars of his time, but also in what we would to-day call Romance linguistics. Many of his unpublished hypotheses were to be re-discovered or confirmed later by influential scholars. Granted that he concentrated initially on the classics, one should not suppose, as some critics have done, that young Giacomo completely neglected or even despised Italian literature. On the contrary, his early verse shows how much he had learned from the Italian poetic tradition, chiefly from the sixteenth to the eighteenth century (Caro, Zappi, Frugoni, Granelli, Varano, Roberti, Fantoni) not to mention minor poets from Piceno, his own region, and some of the earlier classics. His poetic exercises are a valuable document of his poetic apprenticeship. It would be wrong to look back at them from the vantage point of the *Canti* to discover in them signs of precocious greatness. It is much more sensible to take them for what they are, looking forward to the mature writer who would develop in a few years' time. The Jesuits' method of learning by rote, the basis of contemporary education, could, and did, turn many a pupil into an obedient dullard, *perinde ac cadaver*. It could also develop and strengthen the memory of a boy like Giacomo who would persist in stretching all the other faculties of his mind. His memory was outstanding, and things he had only superficially studied would often be subconsciously retained. When he wrote *Appressamento della morte* his immediate literary model had not been Dante but Alfonso Varano's *Visioni* (possibly also Monti's *Bassvilliana*), and he had read Dante only once. Nevertheless the number of images that can be traced back to that single reading of the *Divine Comedy* is quite large.

The scientific component in Giacomo's education and culture should not be underestimated (as it unfortunately has been). As a child he studied quite a lot of arithmetic, geometry and what was then called 'natural philosophy', i.e. science. He was always interested in scientific matters and in recent technological discoveries. His *Storia dell'Astronomia* ranged from the origins of astronomy in classical and eastern antiquity (he did not forget the Chinese!) to up-to-date news on the researches by Piazzi, Schröter, Olbers, Gauss, Harding and Herschel. It dealt not only with astronomy proper but also with matters pertaining to scientific methodology, religion, and the history of comparative traditions. It ended with a bibliography of primary sources (many more secondary references appear in the text or in footnotes) comprising over 300 works by 230 authors or editors: a feat even for a formidable researcher like Leopardi who could often absorb books at the rate of about one a day (as can be deduced from his reading list for June and July 1823) (1, 373). A similar wealth of references is included in the shorter essay *Sopra gli errori popolari degli antichi*, pointing to Giacomo's interests in the fields one would define to-day as ethnology and anthropology. Giacomo's belief, typical of the Enlightenment philosophy he had absorbed, in the need for a scientific and rational approach to truth, together with his understanding of man's need for mythical and metaphysical thought, would bear much fruit in a few years' time.

The youthful Giacomo did not neglect history or contemporary events. His oration celebrating Murat's defeat at Tolentino is commonly judged an immature echo of his father's reactionary feelings, praising as it does 'the paternal administration of beloved legitimate Sovereigns' (1, 872, 2). But there is more to it than juvenile rhetoric. It opens with an attack on Napoleonic despotism, not in the name of an abstract ideal of freedom, but because of its concrete administrative and organizational mismanagement and extortionate taxation (the words *amministrazione, organizzazione, sistema*, occur frequently in the first few paragraphs). His criticism of Murat's government was well-founded and not merely prompted by reactionary considerations. It was, on the contrary, inspired by Foscolo's *Le ultime lettere di Jacopo Ortis*, in particular the letter of 4 December 1798 (1, 363, 2). The maxim 'let us forgo the glitter and stick to substance' is one Leopardi was to practice throughout his life.

Giacomo's philosophical education was, of course, based on the formal and rhetorical 'philosophy' of the Jesuit schools, consisting of logical and moral-theological disputations. The boy paid due homage to it by debating questions taken from Father Odoardo Del Giudice's *Logicae et Ontologiae Eclecticae Elementa ad usum studiosae juventutis*, and Father François Jacquier's *Institutiones philosophicae ad studia theologica potissimum accommodatae*, and by writing essays on subjects such as 'whether idleness or toil is more harmful to man', 'whether poverty is more useful to man than riches', or 'whether animals have a soul'. The names of Spinoza, Hobbes, Maupertuis, Rousseau, Bayle and Helvétius, appear as those of authors to be refuted in the name of Truth and the Catholic Religion: their teachings however had considerable influence on the subsequent development of Leopardi's thought.

About this development Giacomo himself provided some useful information. In his fourth letter to Pietro Giordani (30 May 1817) after mentioning his search for 'the most peregrine and recondite erudition' between the ages of 13 and 17, he wrote:

> Almost without realizing it, I have been devoting myself for one-and-a-half years to literature, which I had previously neglected; and all those compositions of mine which you have read, and others you have not yet seen, have been written during this time. (1, 1029, 2)

Later (*Zib.* 1741, 19.9.1821) he explained:

> Circumstances led me to study languages and classical philology. They alone formed my taste: I therefore spurned poetry. Of course, I did not lack imagination, but I did not realize I was a poet until I read many Greek poets. (My passage, however, from erudition to beauty was not sudden but gradual; that is, by beginning to notice in the ancients something more than I had done before ... The same can be said of my passage from poetry to prose and from literature to philosophy.)

One of the things he had sent Giordani was the *Inno a Nettuno*, the forged antique. 'Here', writes J. H. Whitfield, 'we can find him putting to a different use what he had culled before from the Fathers of the Church in condemnation of the manifold loves of Neptune.

What *was* ancient error can now become poetic enthusiasm'. The 'peregrine and recondite erudition' filling several pages of faked 'notes' was also put to the service of literary beauty, even if the balance still leant on the side of *ingegno* [ingenuity] rather than *fantasia e facoltà poetica* [imagination and poetic faculty] [1, 304, 2].

The time had come for Giacomo to give a coherent intellectual shape and ideological function to all the notions he had absorbed during those seven and more years of intense study. As in 1812 he had outpaced Don Sanchini's teaching skills, so by 1816 he had outgrown Monaldo's ability to be his mentor and guide. He needed a new intellectual father figure. He began looking for one. His collected letters provide evidence of his search. He tried first a friend of his uncle Carlo Antici, the Abbé Francesco Cancellieri, who had mentioned Giacomo's name in his *Dissertazione intorno agli uomini dotati di gran memoria* [Dissertation on Men Gifted With A Great Memory], and had shown Akerblad his philological writings. Unfortunately Cancellieri, Giacomo soon found out, was *un coglione*, 'a flood of twaddle, the most boring and exasperating man on this Earth: he speaks of absurdly frivolous things as if they were extremely interesting, and of the most important things with the greatest possible coldness; he smothers one in compliments and extravagant praise' (Letter to Carlo, 25.11.1822; 1, 1130, 1). He then turned to Angelo Mai, but his relationship with Mai was not to be a particularly happy one. On 21 February 1817, he sent copies of his translation of the second book of the *Aeneid*, published in Milan by Antonio Fortunato Stella, to Mai, Vincenzo Monti and Giordani. Monti and Mai sent the unknown admirer the sort of courteous reply that would please and flatter him without actually suggesting that they wished to cultivate his friendship. Giordani's reply was of a different sort. It consisted of two letters. The first one was sober and reserved in tone: a first cautious step exploring the possibility of further correspondence. Giordani had not known who sent him the book, and why, and he really wanted to know. Almost to counterbalance this cautiousness, the letter contained a personal note, a reference to his own troubles and to the illness of his father. Less than a week later Giordani sent a second letter, showing that in the meantime he had taken the trouble to find out who Giacomo Leopardi was, and that, 'believing young men to be good, truthful and easily affectionate', he wished to reciprocate Giacomo's feelings with equally sincere warmth and affection. In this second letter Giordani touched upon two points that were dear to Leopardi: the role of literature in the regeneration of Italian society (and the responsibility of noblemen to educate themselves to that end), and the function of translations (which Giacomo had discussed in his two unpublished articles the previous year). Giacomo was overjoyed. Here was a man 'whom *he* could hope to have from now on as a teacher', an ardent wish he had cherished for a long time (Letter of 21.3.1817; I, 1019). But what he really needed was not so much a teacher (and Giordani was quick to disclaim the title) as somebody whose opinions would confirm and strengthen his own, who would make him feel intellectually mature and emotionally secure.

Giordani was that man. He was two years older than Monaldo. He had once defined himself 'azionista nel gran traffico odierno delle opinioni' [a shareholder in the big business of ideas]. He was a first-rate classical scholar, one of the few in his time who knew Greek. He constantly championed the most radical views of the Enlightenment. He was a staunch anticlerical and a liberal. He was against the prevailing Jesuit system of education: if some of his educational ideas seem rather naive and dated today it is only because they have been put forward repeatedly by many wise teachers at least from the Renaissance onwards without ever being put into practice by the educational establishment. He was, in short, the opposite of Monaldo. Giacomo chose Giordani as a friend and father substitute. Like Giacomo, Giordani was against glitter and pretence, and preferred to stick to substance. He campaigned vigorously for his ideas during his life, and suffered persecution and even imprisonment because of them. A well-known prose writer, he was not however so famous as Monti and Mai. Giacomo selected him as one of the repipients of his translation on the strength of some articles he had written for the *Biblioteca Italiana* (which was soon to dispense with his collaboration on political grounds).

In order to receive the benefit of his new mentor's understanding and considered advice, Giacomo had necessarily to give him a full account of himself, his life, his projects, his problems, his hopes. He had therefore to carry out nothing less than a complete and detailed self-analysis, which took him as much time as the previous period of hard study. The analysis began with 'a volume, not a letter' addressed to Giordani on 30 April 1817; followed on 30 May by another letter, shorter than the previous one but quite long by normal standards. The next 'confession' to Giordani came, after two short letters, on 8 August. At some time between those two dates Giacomo must have decided that, if he had to explain himself to Giordani, he had better first explain himself to himself. He began to do so in a diary which he later called *Zibaldone* (a word meaning 'hotchpotch', 'medley', which he had probably learned from Vogel, and of which he was reminded by his uncle Carlo Antici in a letter of 9 December 1818). The greater part of this journal was written in two years: 1853 pages in 1821 and 1344 pages in 1823. Giosué Carducci, chairman of the editorial commission that published it in 1898–1900, defined it 'an organic encyclopaedia' of Leopardi's thought. It contains not only a large number of autobiographical remarks and philosophical reflections but also comments on his reading, notes for future essays or poems, linguistic and philological observations. Entries are often cross-referenced backwards and forward (e.g. from p.95 to 12, and from 30 to 3441). Arguments are systematically developed (theoretically as well as stylistically) over long periods. Ideas are tried out for the first time, which will reappear later, more concisely and elegantly written, in works intended for publication. As his 'system' of thought became better defined and the need to develop it further grew less pressing, Leopardi compiled between 11 July and 14 October 1827, a detailed analytical index of the first 4295 pages (out of a total of 4526), presumably in order to review his thoughts and facilitate his use of the *Zibaldone* as a reference work. This index is, of course, far less complete and systematic than those compiled by modern editors, but it is by no means superseded by them; it often groups ideas under headings that are different from those of modern indexes, and shows what subjects Leopardi himself considered to be the most important in his 'system'.

The functional and practical aspects of the *Zibaldone* can be completely missed if one looks at it only from the point of view of its literary beauty, or studies it merely as a source of the *Canti* and *Operette morali*, and as evidence of the poet's culture. The *Zibaldone* was a powerful intellectual tool for Giacomo's own use, and it also enables us to understand his views. But it does more than this. The dialogue Leopardi the writer had with Leopardi the reader often sounds like a dialogue he might be having with us, like his unwritten *Letter to a young man of the twentieth century*. Many of the issues he raised are still very much alive to-day.

3. From Erudition to Poetry

The *Zibaldone* opens with the words: 'Beautiful mansion. Dog at night from cottage, as traveller passes by'. Seven lines of verse follow, describing a moonlit courtyard, with the noise of a cart and the jingling of the harness bells coming from one main road. Then, introduced by the words *'Onde Aviano, raccontando una favoletta, dice...'* [Hence Avianus, telling a story, says...], follows the fable of a woman who threatened her child saying that she would give him to the wolf if he did not stop crying. The child fell asleep, but the woman would never have put her threat into effect in any case, and the foolish wolf who waited all day for the child to be given to him had to go home without his supper.

The question is: why *onde*? There is no apparent logical link between the verse and the fable from a little known fifth century Latin author. But there are hidden connections. Avianus's story had been mentioned at the end of chapter 8 of *Saggio sopra gli errori popolari degli antichi* in a context blaming both the ancient parents and the modern, who should know better, for frightening children with terrifying stories at bedtime, when the darkness and silence of the night and subsequent dreams would conspire to leave an indelible impression on their imagination. But children's fears, however terrifying, often have no basis in reality; and men's fears, Lucretius tells us, are often no better founded than children's (1, 804). In fact Avianus's story is a cautionary tale for wolves, not for children, and has a reassuring ending. There is comfort in knowing that what could be construed as threatening is actually harmless: the howling at night does not come from the big bad wolf but from the cottage dog, the grinding noise is not made by a Stryx but by a moving cart. Reassurance, for both children and grown-ups, comes from seeing that what we feared is not to be feared. Pleasure arises out of the cessation of anxiety: 'piacer figlio d'affanno', Leopardi will write in *La quiete dopo la tempesta* twelve years later. And the last three of the seven lines of verse in *Zib.* 1 point directly to ll.22–4 of this poem; whereas the moonlit landscape of the first four reminds one of *La sera del dì di festa* (1820?) in which the poet contrasts the serenity of the night sky with his own *affanno* [anxiety]; and the silence of the night, highlighted by some distant voice or song, with the infinity of the past in which the clang and clamour of dead civilizations, like the Romans', are drowned (*Zib.* 50).

Onde is therefore a surface sign of the deep connection between classical erudition, represented by Avianus, Lucretius and the Romans, and the poetry of the *Canti*. Formally it is a syntactic and logical 'operator' or device, seemingly misused in this case; semantically, it has profound emotional reverberations. It is as if Leopardi wished at the same time to express the apparent absurdity of moving from the study of dead languages to the writing of living poetry, and to point out the mysterious fact of his passage from erudition to art. The discovery of art (not merely other people's, but one's own creative ability) consisted, for Leopardi the poet as for all other great artists, in realizing (both 'becoming aware of' and 'making real') the possibility of expressing deep emotional contents by means of rationally decodable surface forms, like words, rhythms, tunes, shapes. Such a realization was all the more important for a person like Leopardi, who was repressed and starved of affection and had little or no emotional outlets because of family and social reasons. Let me repeat here that I am not interested in a psychological reconstruction of Leopardi's childhood and adolescence. My main aim is to emphasize the strong emotional basis of his erudite researches, of his 'mad and desperate studies' that were his only outlet, in order to clarify their re-conversion into poetry.

You may ask, at this point (and particularly later, when considering some of my analyses of the *Canti*) whether I am not reading into Leopardi's text more than is actually there. Of course, my analyses may seem unconvincing; but, if so, it should be because they are seen to be flawed and inconsistent, and not because of the fear that I may be putting in the poet's mind ideas that do not appear to be there. That would be practically impossible, since a poet's mind is an inexhaustible repository of ideas, only a few of which are actually conscious. It would be like presuming that any English words that might come into one's mind are not included in the Oxford Dictionary: they are. Writing poetry, like most other human actions, involves a great deal of automatism. When we speak, walk or drive a car, we are not conscious of the staggering complexity of our psychomotory skills, of the incalculable number of stored and received bits of information that our brain processes in a few microseconds, accepting some, rejecting others, memorizing a number for further use. If we had to perform such actions consciously, deliberately reflecting on everything we do, we would become nearly paralyzed. Similarly if a poet had to be fully and rationally aware of every emotion, memory, traditional element, or linguistic device that goes into his poetry, he would be unable to write at all. Most of what one can discover in a poem, therefore, was not intentionally 'put there' by the poet, it does not 'appear to be there' on the surface, and is revealed either by subconscious resonances in the reader's mind or by a critical analysis based on those subconscious resonances. To borrow some models from present-day linguistics, the task of the critic is to find the rules that generate the surface structure of a poem through a complex transformation of its deep semantic structure. It would be wrong to suppose that, given the postulated richness of ideas in the poet's mind, 'anything goes' in the critical operation: the rules must be clear, simple and rigorously constructed.

I have spoken of Leopardi's 'passage' from erudition to art. Words like 'passage', 'conversion' and 'shift' are necessarily imprecise. One tends to interpret them as if they referred to a succession of different self-contained states. Variations in a writer's make-up are usually perceived as occurring along a time-axis, and contrasting ideas are understood as the necessary result of an evolutionary process. But we often forget that, if a man's life appears to unfold through successive stages when seen from the outside, his conscience develops in a sort of continuous present, his mind has access to all the past time-segments stored in his memory, and his unconscious lies outside and beyond time. What may appear as a series of different states are in fact overlapping stages of a continuum of experience that thrives on the dynamic stimulus of contrast and contradiction: particularly so in Leopardi's case, as we shall see in chapter 9. The evolutionary-chronological model of a writer's intellectual development can be useful, but it must not be taken too literally.

What one witnesses in Leopardi's formative years leading to the crises of 1816 (his passage from erudition to poetry) and 1819 (his further 'conversion from poetry to philosophy'), which we shall examine later in greater detail, is a gradual shift from a non-scientific, or pre-scientific, world-view to a scientific and materialistic one. This led him inevitably to the abandonment of religion, which he confessed in his letter to De Sinner quoted in chapter 1 (p. 5). Brought up in an atmosphere where all the values of the past were cherished, in which education was a sort of ritual performance, and the vision of the world was a strongly authoritarian one,

Giacomo developed in his childhood a form of religious devotion. According to Monaldo, he would not walk over floor joints out of respect for the Holy Cross; but Monaldo did not know that Giacomo was performing the almost universal compulsive ritual by which a child symbolizes his grudging acceptance of externally imposed rules and principles of behaviour (including compulsory religious observance), translating into action the metaphors of 'toeing the line' and 'not overstepping the mark'. Religion continued to play a symbolic and ritual role for Giacomo, long after he had rejected it as a means to understand life. Perhaps for this reason he associated it with death: he took Holy Communion as late as 1828 after hearing of his brother Luigi's death (1, 1314, 1), and used to say special prayers—*tridui e novene*, according to a letter of 1832 (1, 1386, 2)—that he too might be released from a painful and wretched existence. Religious festivals, frequently mentioned in the letters and the *Zibaldone*, were important probably because they were enjoyed as family celebrations and reminded him of home. Their mention should not be construed as a sign of religious persuasion: Leopardi used this date style at the end of *Zib.* 2381–4, some of the most polemical pages he ever wrote against the Christian religion.

The *Saggio sopra gli errori popolari degli antichi* (an essay very dear to Leopardi, since he planned two new versions of it, the latest in 1829, see *Zib.* 4484) combined veneration for the classical traditon, fascination for myths and rites, and religious devotion. In this essay Leopardi's enlightened ideas are not so much the product of eighteenth-century free-thinking rationalism as of religious orthodoxy. He was under the influence of the Catholic enlightenment, represented by moderately forward-thinking Jesuits like Roberti, by the Bolognese scientific circle of Eustachio Manfredi, Francesco Maria Zanotti and Luigi Palcani, and by one of Manzoni's teachers, Father Francesco Soave, to mention just a few writers whose works Leopardi knew well and quoted. Their influence ought to be more carefully studied. The method Leopardi suggested to dispel those ancient superstitions was to replace them with religion. But this was a dangerous method, for superstition, as he well understood, is a degeneration of religion, a sort of extension of virtuous belief beyond what it is reasonable to believe; which can only mean that they are similar in kind and that the criterion to distinguish between sane and misleading beliefs must be external to both. 'Only Science can establish the precise point beyond which the effects of virtuous belief must not extend' (1, 866, 2). The way was therefore open to all those truth-seeking methods Leopardi hinted at in the *Saggio*: critical research, abandonment of preconceived ideas, rational thought. But he himself could not engage in yet another round of scholarly researches, after those seven years of erudition, at the expense of his emotions and imagination full of all those 'delectable errors' of the ancients. How ancient errors turned into poetic enthusiasm is clarified by the early pages of the *Zibaldone*. Leopardi's interest in *errori popolari* remained alive a long time. According to *Zibaldone* 4484 he was planning to write a new version of his *Saggio* as late as 1829.

Avianus's story was followed by some reflections on the proper object of art. They are more modern in substance than their traditional form could lead one to believe. Pleasure in art does not arise from a metaphysical and unrealistic idea of beauty, but from the way the artist realizes his depiction of truth, which may include (as the Romantics were discovering) ugly and unpleasant aspects of reality. What matters is not so much what the artist imitates but how he does it. Art is, of course, socially useful, but that is not its primary function. Subsequent pages raise and discuss the issues of the degeneration of Italian literature, the relativity of taste and aesthetic judgements, the function of tradition which must be neither slavishly followed nor presumptuously rejected, the use of neologisms in translation, the peculiar characteristics of French language and literature. Then, halfway through page 14, almost as if Leopardi had suddenly felt the need to reflect on his very act of reflecting upon art, the words:

> A great truth, but one must consider it carefully. Reason is the enemy of all greatness. Reason is the enemy of nature: Nature is great, Reason is small. I mean that the more a man will be dominated by Reason, the less he will be—or the more difficult he will find it to be—great: for few men can be great (and perhaps none in the arts and poetry) unless they are dominated by illusions.

Illusione is a word occurring in Foscolo's *Sepolcri* (mentioned by Leopardi in *Zib.* 13), whose meaning Foscolo himself had defined in a passage of *Le ultime lettere di Jacopo Ortis* (which Leopardi was reading at the time, see *Zib.* 58). The italics are Foscolo's.

> *Illusions*! cries the philosopher.—Well, is not everything illusion? Everything! Happy were the ancients who believed themselves worthy of the kisses of the immortal goddesses from Heaven; who spread divine light over the shortcomings of men, who found *Beauty* and *Truth* in cherishing the idols of their

imagination. *Illusions*! and yet without them I would feel life only as pain, or (what frightens me even more) as stiff and boring indolence. (Part I, 15 May 1798)

Art, and poetry in particular, consists in expressing in a striking and imaginative form one's emotional 'content'. But to theorize about one's own emotions and investigate them rationally seems to diminish their forcefulness. The advancement of philosophical knowledge and psychological analysis ends by weakening the illusions through the revelation of their poetic and emotional function. 'How can they be durable and forceful enough', asked Leopardi, 'once they have been revealed for what they are?' He found himself in a quandary. The forcefulness and function of illusions are revealed through rational processes, but reason, as Leopardi had already recognized at the end of the *Saggio*, destroys them, and their indispensable function. There was only one way out of the impasse, that is to entrust the revelation and celebration of illusions to poetry: to use a type of discourse which on the one hand embodied order, regularity, respect for tradition, logical meaningfulness, rationality (in short, the qualities associated with classical form), and on the other continually drew attention to the disorder of the emotions, the difficulty of reducing life to regular patterns, the need to deviate from accepted rules, and enhanced the semantic ambiguity inherent in living creative language (that is, the discoveries of Romanticism). This will help us to understand why Leopardi became increasingly concerned with the relationship between philosophical and poetic discourse, and why he was able to see through the futility of the Romantic-Classic controversy which he considered pointless and unworthy of intelligent people (I, 439, 2).

4. From Poetry to Philosophy

It may appear surprising that the next thing Leopardi wrote in his *Zibaldone* (pp. 15–21) was a criticism of precisely the kind of poetry one associates with the uninhibited expression of emotions, that is, sentimental Romantic poetry. Two basic meanings of *sentimentale* can be inferred from the end of p. 16:

> …il sentimentale non è prodotto dal sentimentale ma dalla natura *quale ella è*, e la natura *quale ella é* bisogna imitare.

Sentimentale means: (1) the poet's own feelings, i.e. what a sensitive heart may feel under the stimulus of sense impressions (p. 15), and his rational awareness of his own emotions ('that blessed mind of his goes investigating all the secrets of his excitement' p. 17); and (2) the impact poetry has on the readers' emotions ('One must excite this pathetic, this depth of feeling in people's hearts: this is where the real art of the poet lies', p. 15). What the quotation above may therefore be taken to mean is that *sentimentale* (2) is not produced by *sentimentale* (1) but by an immediate and truthful description of Nature itself. The poet should not use his own feelings as material for poetry, because introspection, as we have seen, destroys imagination and fantasy: he should use Nature *nuda*, naked, not interfered with by human reason. *Zib.* 143–4 confirms that *poesia sentimentale* is produced when a poet (Leopardi himself in this case) 'entirely devoted to Reason and Truth', writes poetry *about* his own feelings. But for a more complete typology of poetry one must wait until 1821, when Leopardi will distinguish (*Zib.* 725–35) between: (1) imaginative poetry, typical of the ancients, inspired by Nature and her illusions, capable of arousing strong emotions in its readers; (2) sentimental poetry, typical of the moderns, inspired by the truths of Nature as revealed by Reason; (3) imitative poetry, produced by Leopardi's Italian contemporaries, itself divided into (a) imitation of the imaginative poetry of the ancients, like the classicism of Monti and Arici, and (b) imitation of sentimental poetry, which is the worst kind (because 'one can somehow pretend to have imagination, …never sensitivity') like the verse of some Romantics.

Zibaldone 15–21 was occasioned by an essay written by one of the foremost Romantic critics of the age, Lodovico di Breme, and published in January 1818 by the *Spettatore Italiano*. Leopardi was against Di Breme's theories because they seemed to reduce the essence of poetry to being 'pathetic' or sentimental; that is not about the powerful unreflected natural images that excite human emotions, but about the emotions themselves treated in a cold intellectual way. Leopardi was also against the multitude of mediocre Romantic versifiers because they did nothing but imitate foreign 'sentimental' poets, and therefore turned out to be writers of the worst possible kind of poetry. This side of the argument was developed by him in his *Discorso di un italiano intorno alla poesia romantica* [Essay by an Italian concerning Romantic Poetry], perhaps the most cogent discussion of the Romantic controversy, which remained unfortunately unknown to those involved in the long debate since it was not published until 1906.

A few months before embarking on his meditations leading to the *Discorso*, Leopardi had attempted to re-write his *Saggio sopra gli errori popolari degli antichi*. In the very first page he wrote:

> Popular errors are liked by some because they appear beautiful to them. ... Of course these people know for certain that they are errors, but they would like those errors and false opinions to grow, and remain prosperous and thriving. ... We say to them that, if errors are beautiful, men will derive much beauty from them: here, however, we are not dealing with what is beautiful but with what is useful. (1, 906, 1)

Nevertheless Leopardi was by then much more interested in beauty than in usefulness, and the second draft never went beyond the initial pages. The errors of the ancients were despised by Di Breme because they were due to clumsiness and ignorance; but he failed to see that, once they had become a matter for poetry, the truth criterion (which is essential in intellectual and philosophical matters, where one is dealing with what is useful), no longer applied. Di Breme's theory—Leopardi believed—was not only wrong in preferring sentimental to imaginative poetry; it was also inconsistent because, while he despised classical errors and myths, he accepted contemporary ones. Even worse: while people who liked beautiful ancient errors, as Leopardi did, knew for certain that they were errors, Di Breme and his fellow Romantics took their modern myths (the mutual brotherhood of science and art, the industrial revolution, the miracles of technology, the experimental method, the new discoveries, the progress of civilization) for gospel truths.

As in *Zib.* 15–21, Leopardi considered not only the poet but also the consumers of poetry, the readers whose emotions the poet will arouse. But who read poetry in 1818? Only a small proportion of the educated classes, which themselves were a tiny fraction of the whole population. 'Not since yesterday, or the day before, but for a very long time the common people (*volgo*) have stopped listening to poets.' And, unlike most of his contemporaries for whom the common people were the 'commoners', i.e. the middle classes, and who never seriously thought that literature and poetry should concern the lower classes, Leopardi really had the *volgo*, the *plebe*, the ignorant illiterate masses in mind (for other instances of *volgo* see the letters to Giordani of 30 April and 30 May 1817, where it is synonymous with ignorant masses, plebs, dregs of the populace) (1, 1024, 2; 1031, 2). He deplored the existence of an 'ever growing wall between the writers and the people' in his letter to Montani of 21 May 1819. Like the Romantics, he wanted poetry to be *popolarissima* (1, 917, 2) but unlike them he realized that, in an age in which the common people did not share at all in culture or progress, it was sheer folly to try to make it popular by expressing through it the 'progressive' myths of the élite (which subsequent events indeed showed to have been myths). It was much better to look, as a source of inspiration, to the 'illusions', the 'beautiful errors' common to all men, like religion, but treating them poetically in such a way that only the imagination and not the intellect would be deluded and 'deceived'.

The choice of religion as a popular and immediately comprehensible subject matter for poetry had already been made by Manzoni who was also looking for ways of breaking down the wall between the writers and the people, and had published four of his *Inni sacri* [Sacred Hymns] in 1815. Even if Leopardi had read them as soon as they appeared (we know he read them in 1828), it is unlikely that he would have agreed with Manzoni's devotional ends, incompatible with the principle that religion was acceptable as material for poetry so long as it was treated as an illusion and not as intellectually valid. Two years after the *Discorso* Leopardi, discussing again the question of religious poetry (*Zib.* 285–6) slightly modified his point of view, in that he admitted that poetry 'needs a kind of falsehood that nevertheless may be persuasive': in other words, we may disbelieve mythical poetic inventions, but they must be such that we may be prepared to suspend our disbelief. This was no longer possible in the case of ancient mythology, and of Christianity as well, 'because of the great spread and increase of enlightened ideas'. And yet, if a poet wants to use religious myths, there is only the Christian faith he can turn to, and he can achieve notable results 'if he handles it with judgement, choice and skill'. Between 1819 and 1820 Leopardi himself toyed with the idea of writing some *Inni cristiani*; judging from the notes he left (I, 337) and from the only one he actually wrote (*Inno ai Patriarchi*, Hymn to the Patriarchs, July 1822), a very laborious task considering the unusually large number of corrections, they would have had little to commend them as devotional texts. They were to include constant parallels between classical myths and the Christian religion, notes on the 'crazy idea' that negroes descended from Ham and on the emancipation of slaves, and a rather pessimistic view of redemption in which Christ's sufferings were seen as a pointer not so much to salvation as to the miserable and unhappy condition of all men. But nothing came of that project.

It may be thought from Leopardi's pleas in the *Discorso* for a return to nature that he yearned after an impossible Golden Age and wanted to put the clock back. Nothing could be further from the truth. Precisely because the Golden Age and the perfection of ancient times were delectable errors it was unwise to consider them useful beliefs:

> Nothing could be further from my mind than to vie with those philosophers who shed tears over man becoming civilized and bewailed the change from apples and milk to meat, from tree leaves and animal pelts to clothes, from grottoes and hovels to palaces, and from lonely settlements and woodland to towns.... I do not praise the ancient times, I do not say that those men, those ideas and that way of life were better than in the present.... What I am saying is: that was Nature and this is not, and the poet's task is to imitate Nature. (I, 918, 2; 921, 2)

The beauties of nature, unlike the usefulness of science and the truths of philosophy, are changeless, like nature itself, and have a truly universal appeal. On the other hand the intellectual myths of the cultural élite (that is, of the ruling classes) did nothing but put the poet in chains, in prison, in a straightjacket, and restrict his vision of reality to what could be understood by, and be relevant to, a privileged minority.

> We want Greek, Latin and present poetry and the poetry of all times to share natural, necessary, universal, everlasting contents, not ephemeral ones, nor the arbitrary inventions of men, the particular beliefs and customs of this or that country, the

characteristics and special forms of this or that poet. ... We do not want the poet to be other than a poet: we want him to think, imagine, invent; we want him to be fired with enthusiasm, to have a divinely inspired mind, to have impetus, strength and greatness of emotions and ideas. (1,932,1)

Poetry inspired by nature was therefore, in Leopardi's mind, an essential means for mankind to keep its sanity, to rediscover the primitive world still hidden, among all sorts of encumbrances and obstructions, in the civilized world; and to hear amidst all sorts of noise and distortions the voice of living nature still crying out inside every one of us. This conception excluded all escapism or flight into the past. Civilized man can rediscover nature *only* inside civilization: from a rhetorical question in the *Discorso intorno alla poesia romantica* one can deduce that the primitive world can be seen, inhabited and intimately known only in the civilized world, and nature in the 'unnatural world' (*mondo snaturato*) (1,931, 1). Leopardi, of course, could not have the same understanding as we have to-day of man's alienation, but he used the word long before Marx:

> La nostra condizione oggidì è peggiore di quella dei bruti ... Noi siamo del tutto alienati dalla natura e quindi infelicissimi (Zib. 814). [Our condition to-day is worse than that of the animals ... We are totally alienated from nature, and therefore most unhappy.]

He did not have as clear a perception as many have to-day that the wall between the writers and the people is a class wall, but he came very close to it.

This startling social and political dimension that poetry acquired in the *Discorso* must be understood before one can make any sense at all of its concluding pages, which would otherwise appear to be totally unconnected with what precedes. After the words: 'But now I had enough of writing and you of reading, assuming you had the patience to read so far. Therefore what I have said must suffice' (1, 945, 2) Leopardi abruptly launched into a passionate and emotional appeal to Italian youth, to work for the salvation and greatness of their country. The obvious similarities in contents and form between this peroration and the canzoni *All'Italia* and *Sopra il monumento di Dante* written shortly afterwards (September–October 1818) throw light on the genesis of Leopardi's early political and 'civil' inspiration.

The immediate source of the idea that literature had a social and political function was of course Alfieri, whose tragedies Leopardi had studied at the time of his early dramatic experiments. In November

1817 he had read Alfieri's autobiography, and written a sonnet about it. Alfieri's name appeared both in Leopardi's first letters to Giordani and in the final peroration of the *Discorso*. Superficially Leopardi seemed to share Alfieri's view, stated in *Del Principe e delle lettere*, that the regeneration of Italian society would proceed from the regeneration of Italian literature. But anyone who, like him, had noticed the growing wall separating the writers from the people would know that it was a quixotic view, so long as the vast majority of the population remained illiterate and uneducated. Like Alfieri Leopardi conceived of literature as a form of action; but like Foscolo (*A chi altamente oprar non è concesso fama tentino almen libere carte* 'even if one is not allowed to perform great deeds, one can at least become famous by writing like a free man', Sonnet 12) he thought that literature was only a second best, to be enjoyed only when real action was precluded. A similar idea was expressed by one of the very few contemporaries of Leopardi who had sympathy for him even if he did not share his ideas, Vincenzo Gioberti. 'No one', Gioberti wrote to Roberto D'Azeglio in 1848, 'despises my profession of writer more than I do. If I have practised it so far, if I still do, it is not because I have a great opinion of it, but because men and destiny do not allow me to do anything else'.

Zibaldone 2453, written on 20 May 1822, develops the idea that man is born to act rather than to think. The best use of one's life is not to devote oneself to literature and philosophy, since they are only means to a well-regulated existence (including that of the un-cultivated majority), and means cannot be preferable to the end. No man can be great in literature or philosophy unless he is primarily a man of action, full of life and energy; which was eminently true of Alfieri, as Madame De Staël had pointed out. Six months earlier Leopardi had defined literature as 'the most sterile of all occupations', adding that if it did bear fruit it was only through a sort of confidence trick (*Zib.* 1787–8).

This conception of literature can be traced back to the first *canti* written in 1818. It was confirmed in the first draft of the dedication to Count Leonardo Trissino of the *canzone Ad Angelo Mai*; and can be inferred from the choice of the title for an unfinished verse drama Leopardi began to write in 1819. It was a romantic love tragedy loosely inspired by sixteenth-century pastoral and epic poems. The name of the male protagonist, Girone, harked back to Luigi Alamanni's *Girone cortese*, which Leopardi had been reading at the time (*Zib.* 60, 62). Leopardi wanted it to be an example of 'good' sentimental poetry, founded not on the imitation of French classical theatre but directly upon the study of Nature and human emotions (1, 349, 1). He wanted to put into practice what he had just theorized in the *Discorso*, but its title, taken from the name of the female protagonist, *Telesilla*, is significant because that was the name of the sixth-century Greek poetess who defended Argos against Cleomenes, King of Sparta. According to Pausanias her monument portrayed her looking ecstatically at the helmet she was about to put on, while neglecting a pile of books scattered at her feet as if they represented only a small part of her glory (*Zib.* 2676, and *Il Parini, ovvero della gloria*, 1, 118, 2).

The fifty or so pages of the *Zibaldone* following pages 15–21 (which, as we have seen, formed the nucleus of the *Discorso*) contain a large number of seminal ideas. The references to the Spartans at Thermopylae (22, 44), to Petrarch's *All'Italia* (23, 24, 29), to Chiabrera's political poems (24, 27), to Monti's political odes (36, 37) and to Foscolo's *Ortis* (58) are all preparatory to Leopardi's own *canzone All'Italia* (September 1818). Its first prose draft (1, 331–2) is closely related to the final peroration of the *Discorso*, and specifically refers to *Zib.* 22 and 51 on the concept of illusions; it also includes material to be later developed in *Sopra il monumento di Dante* (Sept.–Oct. 1818) and two lines of poetry ('Dopo il tempo sereno / Tempo d'affanno e d'amarezza pieno') containing that most typically Leopardian word *affanno* to be found in nearly all of his poems, and an idea later to be fully expanded in *Il sabato del villaggio*. The final peroration of the *Discorso* was also echoed in the draft of an unwritten poem *Dell'educare la gioventù italiana*, pointing both backward to the second draft of the *Saggio sugli errori popolari degli antichi* and forward to *Nelle nozze della sorella Paolina* (Oct.–Nov. 1821). The same fifty pages of the *Zibaldone* comprise also themes that will later reappear in *Il sogno* (Winter 1820) and *Le ricordanze* (Aug.–Sept. 1829) (*Zib.* 36, 47) and *La sera del dì di festa* (Spring 1820) (*Zib.* 50–51); references to Goethe's *Die Leiden des jungen Werthers* which, as Giorgio Manacorda has convincingly demonstrated, may be considered a source of many passages of *L'infinito* (1819), *Il sogno*, *La vita solitaria* (1821), *Le ricordanze*, perhaps even of *La ginestra* (1836); and many overt or hidden quotations from the works of Madame de Staël, which had a profound influence on Leopardi's thought. In *Zib.* 1742 (following on the quotation in chapter 2, page 12 of this book) Leopardi wrote:

> Having devoted myself entirely and with great pleasure to *belles lettres*, I despised and hated philosophy. The *Meditations*,

which our age likes so much, bored me. According to the
usual prejudices I believed I was born to literature, imagination,
emotions, and that it would be altogether impossible for me to
apply myself to the contrary faculties, that is, reason, philosophy, mathematical abstraction, and to do so successfully. I did
not lack the ability to reflect, concentrate, compare, reason
things out, combine ideas; I was capable of depth etc., but,
until I read certain works by Madame de Staël I did not think I
could be a philosopher.

One must not take Leopardi too literally. Pascal's *Pensées*, often
quoted in the previous pages of the *Zibaldone*, did not bore him. The
passage from poetry to philosophy was not a radical one, since it was
precisely in 1819, date of his alleged 'conversion' (*Zib.* 144), that he
began to write his first important poems.

Madame de Staël points the way out of this apparent contradiction. The study of her works showed Leopardi that there was no
real incompatibility between imagination and emotions on the one
hand, and the 'contrary faculties' of reason, philosophy and mathematical abstraction on the other. A persuasive opponent of intellectual pigeon-holing and of rigid boundaries between the various
intellectual disciplines, Madame de Staël, spent a great deal of her
energies demonstrating how to use varied and diverse approaches,
how to employ concepts and facts from different methods and
sources to arrive at a better understanding of the history of ideas and
the cultural development of mankind, with a view to improving
the present state of society. In her treatise *De l'influence des passions
sur le bonheur des individus et des nations* [On the Influence of Passions
on Individual and Social Happiness, 1796] she had tried to solve the
dichotomy between nature (emotions, sensitivity) and reason that
was soon also to occupy Leopardi's mind. So long as he identified
philosophy with pure mechanical rationalism, suppression of emotions (*Zib.* 111, 116), sterile speculation incapable of promoting
social change (*Zib.* 160-1) and *esprit géometrique*, or came across
philosophers embodying or supporting that view, he could not fail
to be bored and repelled by philosophy. What Leopardi would have
liked, what he considered necessary for a moral, political and cultural regeneration of society was 'a sort of superphilosophy which,
knowing the whole and the essence of things, would bring us back to
Nature' (*Zib.* 115). This was precisely the view of philosophy
Madame de Staël had put forward. She had clearly stated that
philosophy should not be divorced from sensitivity; she had shown

how philosophy, by helping one to grow out of the beautiful illusions of youth, induces in one's spirit a happy melancholy which makes one more sensitive to nature and brings about a sort of correspondence between natural phenomena and one's innermost feelings; she had emphasized the emotional satisfaction, enhancing one's self-awareness, arising out of the combination and development of abstract ideas. In her book, *De l'Allemagne*, which was first published in 1810, she had repeatedly stressed the need for a philosophy that would concern itself with totalities of experience and with the relationships between the various aspects and parts of such totalities; and had extended this concern from the relationship between the data of our rational experience to all those things that cannot yet be rationally comprehended:

> What we call errors and superstitions may pertain to laws of the Universe as yet unknown to us.... It does not follow, of course, that we should renounce the experimental method so necessary in science. But why should we not establish, as a supreme guiding principle of that method, a more comprehensive philosophy, embracing the Universe in its totality, and not neglecting the nocturnal aspect of Nature (*le coté nocturne de la nature*) in the hope that it may shed some light there?

And, conscious that 'the nocturnal aspect of Nature' was a poetic image, she continued:

> Poets could find in science a crowd of useful ideas if these ideas were all interrelated through this philosophy of the universe, and if this philosophy, instead of being abstract, were animated by the inexhaustible sources of the emotions. The universe resembles more a poem than a machine; and if one should choose in order to understand it, between imagination and mathematics, imagination would get nearer the truth. But, once more, we must not choose, since it is the totality of our moral being that must engage in such an important meditation.

It was precisely along these lines that Leopardi's thought developed (and let me repeat once more that this development must not be taken in a chronological, linear sense, but rather as the gradual focussing and sharpening of a complex image in all its contrasting and complementary aspects). At various stages in the *Zibaldone* (111, 1231, 1360, 1383) he rejected the formal rationalistic abstract 'geometrical' conception of philosophy as being incompatible with natural emotions and poetry; at the same time he came to realize that a different conception was possible. He hoped for a 'superphilosophy' capable, through a detailed analysis of the connections between ideas, of bringing us nearer to nature, and stimulating and freeing our emotions and poetic imagination (*Zib.* 114–15, 947–8, 1360, 1383, 1650, 1833–40, 3237–45, 3382–6). For Leopardi the 'passage from poetry to philosophy', where he had as mentor not only Madame de Staël but also Francesco Maria Zanotti (see p. 63), could only be the discovery of a new notion of philosophy that would include and promote poetry. The qualities that make a great poet

> are all contained in, and derived from, his ability to discover relations between things; even the slightest and remotest connections, even of things seemingly the least similar etc. Now this is also wholly true of the philosopher: an ability to discover and understand relations, to connect details together, to generalize. (*Zib.* 1650; 7.9.1821; cp. also *Comparazione delle sentenze di Bruto e Teofrasto*, I, 207–8; *Parini, ovvero della gloria*, ch. VII, I, 126–7).

This is why the year of Leopardi's 'conversion' to philosophy marked also the beginning of his outstanding poetic career.

5. 'Investigation of Relationships'

When Leopardi was writing the canzone *All'Italia*, Italy was in the grip of various authoritarian governments, all subservient to the policies of the Austrian foreign minister Prince Klemens von Metternich who hoped to eradicate from Europe the plague of French-inspired liberalism and the memory of Napoleon's political reforms. This attempt to put the clock back, that goes by the name of Restoration, was only partially successful. Leopardi's generation was poised to begin that long and difficult process of liberation from foreign influences, political unification and acquisition of national identity known as *Risorgimento*, which no amount of police repression could effectively stop. In such a political atmosphere Leopardi's first three *canzoni* were read by his contemporaries as exhortations to action, as inspiration to deeds of patriotic valour. Whether that was what Leopardi really meant is however open to question, as I hope to explain later (p. 36 in this chapter and chapter 6). Let us first devote some time to an equally important question, following from the reconciliation between poetry and a new form of scientific philosophy we discussed in the previous chapter.

The form of Leopardi's first poems can be seen as a structural metaphor of his epistemology. In other words, what Leopardi called *speculazione dei rapporti*, the ability to bring to light the system of relationships between things in nature possessed by philosophers and poets alike, is mirrored in the structure of his poems. The complex web of ideas, references and reminiscences on which his inspiration drew, is paralleled in the poems by an equally complex 'system of relationships', an intricate texture of metrical, lexical and phonetic symmetries, subtle assonances, inner rhymes, overlapping rhythms, at all times sustaining and emphasizing meaning relationships and connections of ideas within the poems.

Let us take a closer look at *All'Italia*. Some of its various cultural and literary sources have already been mentioned in the previous chapter (to Petrarch and Foscolo one should add Sannazaro, Rucellai, Della Casa, Chiabrera, Guidi). This canzone is composed of seven stanzas of twenty lines each. The number seven reappears in other subpatterns of the poem. The stanzas are grouped in pairs, each with a different metrical structure. In the odd ones there are seven lines of seven syllables each (3, 4, 8, 11, 16, 17, 19); and in the even ones only six (2, 5, 10, 12, 14, 19); so that, apart from line 19, no heptasyllabic lines occupy the same positions. The rhyme scheme falls into three groups of lines: the first seven, with three paired rhymes and one 'free' (A B C D A B C in odd stanzas, A B C D A B D in even ones); the next seven with a similar pattern (E F G E F H G); and the last six which however fit into a hidden seven-line pattern by having line 16 rhyming with 13 in the previous group (I H J K I K). Many of the rhymes are reinforced by vocalic assonance, that is, by other words having the same vowels and stress pattern. Here assonance is based on the pair E...O in the first stanza (*veggio, chiedo al cielo, questo è peggio, velo*) A...O in the second (*pianto, vanto, quando, brando*), A...I in the third (*armi, timballi, parmi, cavalli, lampi campi, acciari, cari*), O...E in the fourth (*morte, gloriose, forte, generose, voce, feroce*). If we define 'assonance' the presence of the same sounds (same vowels but different consonants, or the other way round) within identical stress patterns, and 'alliteration' the frequent repetition of the same sound, we notice vocalic alliteration in lines 31–3 of the second stanza (qual *arte* o qual *fatica*/o qual *tanta possanza*/valse a spogliarti il *manto*'). The same stanza offers an interesting combination of alliteration (*fosser, fonti*, 21), consonantal assonance (*fonti-pianto* 21–2, *danno-donna* 23–4, *rimembrando-grande* 26–7), vocalic assonance (A...O: *pianto, danno, rimembrando, vanto, manto, quando*), inner rime (*rimembrando-brando* 26–30, *vanto-manto* 26–33, *fato-prostrato* 124–36), stress change in anaphora (*dov'è* 28, *dove* 29), inversion (*io solo* 37, *sol'io* 38). The word *donna* appearing before the caesura of line 24 reminds the reader of the previous stanza where it is found in a similar position (10). Other words establishing references to other stanzas are *pianto* (22, 100) *armi* (29, 37, 41, 88) *pugna* and its cognates (36, 44, 51, 53) *sangue* (40, 9, 133), to mention only those linking the second stanza to the others. Other key Leopardian words and expressions to be found in later poems are *misero, acerbo fato, duro* and *affanno* (the latter occurs 36 times in the *Canti*).

Such a network of relationships is not random: it links together words that are particularly significant. In the first stanza of *Sopra il monumento di Dante*, to give another example, rhymes, vocalic harmonies and assonances are a function of the conceptual links and oppositions in its structure. The Italian people (*genti*) will come together (*raccolga*) in peaceful unity when their minds (*menti*) wil wake up from their slumber (*sopor*) and turn (*rivolga*) with reverence (*onor*) to the examples of the past. They should turn to the immortal men (*immortali*) of past ages since Italy itself is bereft of such men (*altrettali*) in the present time. This last idea is given extraordinary relief by a series of assonances and alliterations connecting it with the expression of shame and indignation for the country's present state. The three syllables of *vedove* (9) are echoed by three stress-bearing syllables in the following line (ne *v'é* chi *d'onorar* ti si con*vegna*) where the secondary stress corresponds to the unstressed syllable in *vedove*. Its last word is echoed by the rime *disdegna*, harmonizing with *convegna* (10) and *vergogna* (15). *Disdegna* is part of a sybilant-dental alliteration (*di te stessa ti disdegna*/che *senza sdegno omai la doglia è stolta*), while *vergogna*, besides being a part of the *gn* consonantal harmony, fits into a system of correspondences based on initial *v-* (*vedove, v'è, volgiti* twice, *volta*). *Sdegno*, the word that sums up both sybilant-dental and palatal-nasal alliterations, rhymes with *ingegno*, found in a similar position before the caesura of the first line of the next stanza. The two words are linked again by an inner rhyme in lines 42–6. *Vergogna* reappears in line 23. The final lines of the first stanza (...ti punga una volta/ pensier...) are echoed by a similar *p* alliteration at the beginning of the third stanza (Voi spirerà...ed acri punte premeravvi al seno) which preserves the image of 'conscience pricking'. One could continue with this type of analysis taking examples from this and other poems.

Just as important as the system of echoes contained within each poem is the network of connections between individual poems. Shortly after writing *Sopra il monumento di Dante*, Leopardi composed two canzoni he later excluded from the collected *Canti*. They were entitled *Nella morte di una donna fatta trucidare col suo portato dal corruttore per mano e arte di un chirurgo* [On the Death of a Woman whom her Debaucher had murdered by the Hand and Art of a Surgeon with the Child she was bearing] and *Per una donna inferma di malattia lunga e mortale* [For a Woman Ill with a Long and Deadly Disease]. The first one, for which Giacomo had a 'special affection' but of which Monaldo predictably disapproved, was about a twenty-four-year old married woman from Pesaro, Virginia del Mazzo, who had died on 29 January 1819, of the consequences of an abortion performed by the surgeon Angelo Lorenzini at the instigation of her lover, Guerrino Guerrini, who was also her husband's employer. About the same time Leopardi was also thinking of writing 'the story of a poor nun from Osimo who, desperate because she had been forced to take the veil, committed suicide by jumping out of a window at her convent of St Stephen in Recanati' (1, 367, 1). Insofar as his choice of subjects for his poetry was a rejection of classical and 'ancient' subjects, Leopardi was being influenced by the very Romantic theories he had opposed the year before. In 1816 Tommaso Grossi, Manzoni's friend, had written *La fuggitiva*, a poem in Milanese dialect about a girl who followed her lover, an officer in Napoleon's army, as far as Russia. Manzoni would soon be writing about the unhappy Nun of Monza. The early fame of Giovanni Prati was largely due to the scandal caused in 1841 by the publication of *Edmenegarda*, a poem in which he retold the adultery of a well-known Venetian lady. Leopardi had been equally, if not more, daring in his choice of subject well over twenty years before. And yet, like Manzoni, he was not really interested in telling tearful Romantic stories or in exploiting his readers' curiosity for scandalous news items. His acceptance of the Romantic principle of contemporary subject-matter was due to his 'need to make a truly Italian literature as popular as other literatures are in their countries, suitable for women and uneducated people and dear to them', as he wrote in a draft for a treatise *On the Present Conditions of Italian Literature* which he was also planning to write at that time (1, 368–9). The reason for his daring choice was hinted at in the opening lines of the canzone:

Mentre i destini piango e i nostri danni
Ecco nova di lutto
Cagion s'accresce alle cagioni antiche.
[While I lament our destinies and our troubles, behold, a further cause for grief is added to the ancient causes.]

The abortion incident at Pesaro was seen by Leopardi as yet another example of the evils he had denounced in *All'Italia* and *Sopra il monumento di Dante*; a particular case of the general moral stagnation and backwardness of Italy, against which he had already raised his voice in condemnation. The 'investigation of relations' through which poetry and philosophy had become reconciled could not fail to include Leopardi's own relationship to individuals and society. His early poems contain many formal signs of personal involvement: thirty-seven question marks in *All'Italia* and *Sopra il monumento di Dante*; the frequent use of the pronoun *io* (7 times in *All'Italia*, 4 in *Sopra il monumento di Dante*, 13 in *Nella morte di una donna* and 25 in

Per una donna inferma, not counting verbs in the first person and direct forms of address). But since he was painfully aware that his 'investigations' were an inadequate substitute for direct action, his personal involvement with problems he could not hope to solve generated increasing frustration. In the first two poems Leopardi's *io* had mainly an exhortatory and inspirational role: his lonely fight against all enemies and his death for his country (*All'Italia* 37–40) could only be a heroic fantasy. Nicolò Tommaseo took those four lines as an opportunity of venting his sectarian biliousness against a writer who did not share his religious faith. In the entry *procombere* of his *Dizionario della lingua italiana* (which he began publishing in 1856) he wrote:

> It is used by a modern versemonger who said he was ready to die for his fatherland... Since he gave no evidence of being able even to bear his own sorrows in a manly way, his bravado appears to be nothing but rhetorical pedantry.

Tommaseo was wrong in accusing Leopardi of moral weakness; but he accurately sensed the hopelessness pervading those lines. The rhetorical form of all those thirty-seven questions clearly implied that no answer could be expected. Hopelessness turned to frustration as Leopardi no longer faced generalized social marasmus but individual corruption. Somebody might hear his exhortations, from among the youth of Italy; but poetry could not undo the hateful crime of Pesaro. Frustration reached its climax when the speaking *io* had to come to terms with an invisible and invincible enemy, Death, threatening the life of a young woman. The causes for the decadence of Italy and the motives for Virginia's abortion could be understood; but the death of young people (a theme more fully developed in *A Silvia* 1828, *Le ricordanze* 1829, and *Amore e Morte* 1832) cannot be explained away. Nor can it be prevented:

> But can we do nothing for her? For Heaven's sake, I want to go and see whether it's possible, let us consult the physician, some remedy. Nothing. Being poor mortals we cannot do anything against our own and other people's death. And I will see you die, o hapless one,...full of vain anxiety [*affannandomi invano*] because I cannot cannot do anything. (Prose draft, *Per una donna malata,* I, 335, 1)

In the following poem, probably written in September 1819, the changes of form are startling. The first four canzoni had 140, 200, 140 and 151 lines respectively. *L'infinito* [Infinity] is sonnet-size, only 15 lines; and yet, as Anna Dolfi perceptively remarked, it is un *sonetto negato*, an anti-sonnet. The descriptive horizon of the earlier poems is drastically reduced. Complete immobility replaces fretting and frustrated action. The rustle of leaves in the wind is heard instead of the sound of warring armies. Instead of anxious questioning we have complete silence. The rhythmical alternation of hendecasyllables and heptameters gives way to the apparent uniformity of blank verse; but if one rearranges the poem, making line divisions at some of the more conspicuous cesurae, rhythmical variety reappears. The oblique lines below indicate the published line-divisions:

Sempre caro mi fu quest'ermo colle /
E questa siepe che da tanta parte /
Dell'ultimo orizzonte il guardo esclude. /
Ma sedendo e mirando interminati /
Spazi di là da quella
E sovrumani / silenzi
E profondissima quiete /
Io nel pensier mi fingo
Ove per poco / il cor non si spaura.
E come il vento /
Odo stormir tra queste piante, io quello /
Infinito silenzio a questa voce /
Vo comparando: e mi sovvien l'eterno /
E le morte stagioni
E la presente / e viva
E il suon di lei.
Così tra questa / immensità s'annega
Il pensier mio: /
E il naufragar m'è dolce
In questo mare. /

[This lonely hill was always dear to me, and this hedge which shuts off the gaze from such a large part of the furthest horizon. But, sitting in contemplation, I give shape in my thought to endless spaces beyond, silences such as were never experienced by man, and deepest quiet; where the heart is almost overcome by fear. And as I listen to the wind rustling among these plants, I keep comparing this voice to that infinite silence: and I recall eternity, and the dead seasons, and the present living one, and its sound. So in this immensity my thoughts drown, and in this sea shipwreck is sweet to me.]

That this alternative rhythmical pattern is actually hidden in *L'infinito* is proved by the correspondence between lines 17–18 of my re-writing and two pairs of lines taken from *Ad Angelo Mai* (ll. 114–15) and *Il sogno* (ll. 66–7):

> Cosi tra questa immenità s'annega / il pensier mio
>
> In mille vane amentità si perde / la mente mia
>
> Oggi nel vano dubitar si stanca / la mente mia

'Affanno', a word present in all the previous poems, is missing from *L'infinito*: we have instead 'e sovrumani silenzi', 'e profondissima quiete', 'quello infinito silenzio', three identical rhythmical phrases. Even the final image of drowning is devoid of all anxiety. There is no feeling of breathlessness, suffocation or death; rather the wish for a return to the primaeval amniotic fluid from which all life comes, to suffer a sea-change into something rich and strange. This theme is found also in a poem by Luis de Leon, dedicated to Francisco de Salinas, composer and organist in Salamanca about 1557. Here the mystical oceanic feeling is induced by Salinas's music:

> Aqui la alma navega
>
> por un mar de dulzura, y finalmente
>
> en el ansì se anega
>
> que ningun accidente
>
> estraño y peregrino oye y siente.
>
> [Here the soul sails in a sea of sweetness, and there it drowns, so as not to hear or feel any extraneous or distant stimulus.]

There are other similarities. Luis used the *lira* in his poetry, a five-line stanza alternating hendecasyllables and heptameters, a combination of metres of Italian origin he had derived from Garcilaso de la Vega, which, as we know, were also dear to Leopardi. The poetic temperament of Luis, like Leopardi's, was as insensitive to the visible world as is compatible with being a poet, but was endowed with great sensitivity to sounds. Like Luis, Leopardi loved music, which he believed could express vague and indefinite feelings much better than words (*Zib.* 79–80) and 'plunge the listener into a confused abyss of innumerable and indefinite sensations' (*Zib.* 1782). This idea reappears in *Sopra il ritratto di una bella donna scolpito nel monumento sepolcrale della medesima* [On the Portrait of a Beautiful Woman Carved on her own Sepulchral Monument; see p. 105 below for dating], in a group of verses equally reminiscent of Luis de Leon's poem and of *L'infinito*:

> Desiderii infiniti
>
> e visioni altere

crea nel vago pensiere
per natural virtù, dotto concento:
onde per mar delizioso, arcano
erra lo spirto umano
quasi come a diporto
ardito notator per l'Oceano:
ma se un discorde accento
fere l'orecchio, in nulla
torna quel paradiso in un momento. (ll. 39–49)
[A masterly concert has the natural virtue of creating in a
receptive mind infinite desires and lofty visions. Thus the
human spirit wanders through a delightful and mysterious sea,
like a daring sportsman swimming in the Ocean. But if the ear
is struck by a discordant note, that paradise suddenly turns to
nothing.]

It has been argued, on the basis of what was available in Monaldo's
library, that Giacomo could not have read Luis de Leon; but not
enough is known about the books he may have borrowed from other
libraries in Recanati belonging to the Anticis, the Robertis, the Politis,
and from the Spanish Rector of the local Seminary Father Francisco
Serrano, to exclude that possibility, especially considering Giacomo's
extraordinary memory. But what to my mind is more important
than the alleged derivation of images is the question of the cultural
and psychological circumstances of their use, which may throw some
light on the reason why the same images may be used by different
writers at different times. Here I can do no more than suggest a few
lines of inquiry concerning the significance for Leopardi of the sea
image as a powerful archetypal symbol of the unconscious in all its
comprehensiveness, timelessness and undifferentiation; of the womb,
of life itself; and of sound as a gateway to the 'oceanic' feeling of
being dissolved into infinity. 'The spectacle of the sea', wrote
Madame de Staël in Corinne, 'always makes a deep impression. It is
the image of that infinity which unceasingly attracts thought, and
where thought loses itself'.

We may begin to note in this connection (as we did at the end of
chapter 1) the constructive 'poetic' use to which Leopardi put his
physical disabilities and unfortunate circumstances. We know his
eyes were poor, and he was obliged to spend long periods in darkness: unable to rely on his sense of sight he developed his imaginative
vision. Restricted to his cramped horizon of Recanati, he deliberately restricted it even further to escape into infinity. And then he

investigated the connection between those two experiences deducing
from them a complete aesthetic and poetic theory.

Unlike words, or paintings, mere sounds have no representational
value, no 'determinate and finite meaning' (*Zib.* 79). They are therefore much better at expressing vague and indefinite feelings. Sounds
produce inherently greater spiritual effects; emotions derive immediately from them (*Zib.* 157–8). Whereas sounds (and to a lesser
degree smells) are associated with spiritual faculties and imagination,
the other senses have a decidedly material nature. Sight is the most
material of all the senses (*Zib.* 1944), but, since this is a distinction
Leopardi also reserves for reason (*Zib.* 107), there seems to be an
association in Leopardi's mind between the objectifying properties
of sight and the demystifying properties of reason, which is compared
to a lamp throwing its light over Nature (*Zib.* 22). Both good eye-
sight and sharp reasoning eliminate all ambiguities and destroy man's
cherished illusions. In *L'infinito* it would take but a little *accidente
estraño y peregrino* to frighten the heart, but the heart is not frightened.
The poet's ear perceives sounds that help him to control the meditative process and not to cross the thin demarcation line between
ecstasy and anxiety. The rustling of the wind, like the song of the
artisan in *La sera del dì di festa* (see p.51 below) generates a train of
images which are not only poetically realized as complex sound
structures but also seem to minimize the visual element. Some
unusual expressions result: the poet hears the *sound* of seasons, the
sound of ancient peoples, the *noise* of the lost Roman Empire; he
does not *see*, as one would expect, their colours, shapes, events. It is
sight which, in another poem having some formal resemblance to
L'infinito, produces fear; when the eyes move from the contemplation
of the loved object to the depressing spectacle of the desert of life;
and the earth appears uninhabitable, stripped by sight of the infinite
happiness conjured up in the imagination; and the 'sea of being' is
no longer pleasurable but threatening and stormy (*Amore e morte*,
Love and Death, ll. 34–44; see p. 102 below).

Leopardi concerned himself with poetic ambiguity from a very
early stage, in an extremely perceptive note on a poem by Chiabrera,
which, incidentally, tells us a great deal about how one should read
Leopardi's own poems. He thought poetic images should be un-
motivated, without, that is, having a clear semantic rationale; and
that they should appear 'accidental'. In this way their poetic form
would be a structural metaphor of the vague and indefinite emotions
they strive to express (*Zib.* 26). He clearly undestood what, in

modern terminology, we would call the arbitrariness and polysemy of the poetic sign. In January 1820 he clarified his ideas in a page where one catches a reflection of the horizonless landscape of *L'infinito*:

> A country scene...sketched by an ancient poet in a few strokes, without—so to speak—its horizon, aroused in our fantasy that heavenly ripple of confused ideas, bright with an undefinable romantic quality, and that all-too-dear and sweet wandering of the imagination and amazement which used to fill us with ecstasy in our childhood. Modern poets, on the other hand, defining as they do every object and showing its exact boundaries, lack almost completely that infinite emotion, and only arouse instead the limited and circumscribed emotion originating from the knowledge of the whole object...missing the inexpressible delights of the wandering imagination we experienced in our childhood. (*Zib.* 100)

These ideas fitted in very well not only with the criticism of sentimental Romantic poetry that Leopardi had elaborated in his *Discorso*, but also with the distinction that was taking shape in his mind between rational and scientific speculation on the one hand, when words lose their polysemy to become technical terms (*Zib.* 109–11, 1226, 1234–6), and poetry allied to a 'superphilosophy' on the other, where what matters is precisely the imaginative *speculazione dei rapporti*, which scientific terminology restricts and poetic ambiguity necessarily enhances. Leopardi did not reject the use of scientific discourses and scientific terms, which he considered indispensable in certain contexts (*Zib.* 1226, 2721); nor did he equate 'vague' and 'indefinite' with obscure and imprecise. On the contrary, he was concerned with clarity and precision, not only of the philosophical type (consisting in the clear expression of rational ideas) but also of the poetic kind (consisting in the clear expression of unclear states of mind and indefinite emotions) (*Zib.* 1273). For all these reasons vague and partial sense impressions (like restricted or blocked views, distant noises in the dark, 'the very things which are in themselves indifferent to rational man' (*Zib.* 381)) can be very powerful stimuli to poetic imagination. Illusions, which are palpably untrue, are nevertheless the very stuff our emotions feed on, and only to that extent are they real and do they afford us the most substantial pleasure in our life (*Zib.* 51, 90). Pleasure itself can only have an illusory quality: granted that all men tend towards pleasure in general, they can never be satisfied with any particular, real, definable pleasure. Pleasure is therefore infinite and indefinite, hope is always greater than achievement, and imagination is the primary source of happiness (*Zib.* 165–72).

Nearly all these reflections were developed after the composition of *L'infinito*. Unlike the earlier poems, those fifteen miraculous lines had hardly any sources in Leopardi's previous writings. They came to him at the height of a difficult crisis, out of an inner necessity, as a total poetic intuition. Giacomo had for some time been fighting a losing battle to be allowed to travel outside Recanati. His father's obdurate refusals filled him with despair. In the early Summer of 1819 he planned to escape, but could not do so without first obtaining a passport. He asked a family friend, Count Xaverio Broglio d'Ajano, to procure him a travel document for Milan, pretending that his father was in agreement. Monaldo heard about Giacomo's project from Carlo Antici, to whom Marquess Filippo Solari, the Police Chief in Macerata, had innocently written wishing his nephew a happy journey. On Monaldo's request, Solari asked Broglio to send the passport directly to Giacomo's father. Broglio, unsuspectingly complied. Monaldo then informed his son that the passport lay in an open drawer: if he really wished to leave, he could take it. Giacomo was shocked by this moral blackmail: 'It did not please God that they should use force', he wrote to Giordani; 'they have used prayers and protestations of grief. I have no hope left' (1, 1087, 1). Three months later, according to another letter to Giordani, he had touched the bottom of his depression:

> I am so numbed by the nothingness surrounding me that I do not know how I manage the strength to answer your letter of November 1. If I were to go mad at this very moment, I think my madness would consist in my remaining always seated, with glassy eyes, a gaping mouth, my hands between my knees, neither laughing nor crying, without moving unless I was made to. (1, 1089, 2)

This is a precise description of a schizoid state, of complete immobility or 'catatonia' which symbolizes the ultimate rejection of surrounding reality, perceived as 'solid nothingness' (*Zib.* 85). Perhaps Leopardi did actually experience such a state; but what really matters is his use of language to turn an unconscious defence mechanism of the mind into a conscious attitude of the body, through its detailed verbalization. Human beings have since time immemorial attempted consciously to use the body's autonomous defence mechanism to control depression and reduce stress and anxiety through techniques involving sensory deprivation, reduced mobility, often concentration on sounds ('mantras') as a means of deepening meditation. Meditation is after all a sort of deliberately induced catatonic state. We have no reason to suppose that Leopardi was aware of using such techniques, even if he spent much of his time on his own, in silence, often in darkness because of his eye complaints. But we do know that, at the height of his crisis, he wrote a poem which is at the same time a meditation, a description of a meditative process, a therapeutic projection of the poet's fragmented self into a perfect work of art, closing on one of the most powerful 'nirvanic' images known to literature. Thus *L'infinito* appeared at a crucial time in Leopardi's life, as the poetic matrix of a complex speculative system embracing some of his most important ideas. Leopardi recognized this fact by publishing the poem in 1826 as the first six *Idylls* (the others were *La sera del dì di festa, Alla luna, Il sogno, Lo spavento notturno, La vita solitaria*) to which he gave the common date of 1819. 'Idyll' is a Greek word meaning 'small picture', 'little vision', traditionally used by poets and critics to indicate poems presenting in a short compass an idealized or meditative description of everyday life, or expressing a simple but intense emotional state. While one can appreciate the significance of this title, it is also true that *L'infinito* is much more than a 'little vision', a 'musical moment' or an 'album leaf'. It is not the immediate transcription of an intense poetic vision through which the poet freed himself from his philosophical meditations. It is on the contrary the poetic nucleus of those very meditations, the first mature fruit of that *speculazione dei rapporti* through which Leopardi intended that both poetry and philosophy should be generated.

6. The 'Civic Odes' and other Poems

On 4 February 1820 Leopardi sent by registered post to Pietro Brighenti in Bologna the manuscript of the two 'romantic' *canzoni* and of a new one he wanted to be published. Brighenti, with whom Leopardi had been corresponding since September 1818, was a cultivated, resourceful and warm-hearted man, a friend of Giordani's. He was also an informer of the Austrian police. It seems however that he did not perform that unsavoury duty out of malice or political conviction. He was constantly trying to supplement his meagre income as a lawyer, on which he had an ailing wife and two daughters to support, by various part-time or occasional occupations, including those of bookseller, publisher, journalist, impresario; and he probably thought it better that the Austrians should get reports on his friends from himself rather than from some other unsympathetic police spy: which would have happened anyway, and would have been unprofitable for Brighenti and dangerous for his friends. There is in fact no evidence that because of Brighenti's activities either Giordani or Leopardi suffered any harm that they would not have incurred as a result of their openly admitted political opinions. Leopardi was fully aware of the ideological significance of his first published poems, which had been welcomed by the liberals and had failed to please the established authorities. This worried Monaldo, who somehow got wind of Giacomo's intention to publish some new *canzoni* (Brighenti had suggested that Giacomo should reprint with them the first two), and hastened to prevent it. He had however not been able to lay his hands on them and therefore could only make conjectures about their contents from their titles. Of those about the two women, one murdered at the instigation of her lover, the other terminally ill, he predictably disapproved; but he mistakenly thought that *Ad Angelo Mai quand'ebbe trovato i libri di Cicerone della Repubblica* [To Angelo Mai on the Occasion of His Discovery of Cicero's 'Republic'], being dedicated to a respected prelate and about classical philology, would be perfectly innocent. Little did he know, Giacomo wrote to Brighenti on 20 April 'that there is someone who is able to make use of any subject to speak of what matters most to him, and...that under that title lurks a poem full of dreadful fanaticism' (1, 1100, 1). No wonder the report filed with the Austrian police confirmed Giacomo's own judgement, saying that the poem 'stank of that deadly liberalism which seems to have blinded many an unhappy mind in our country', and that it was particularly dangerous since, having been published in a cheap edition, everybody could afford to read it.

Monsignor Angelo Mai was then thirty-eight and had been Chief Librarian of the Vatican Library for about a year. Shortly after taking up his post he discovered that a tenth-century palimpsest contained large fragments of Cicero's *De Republica*, a work the greatest humanists had searched for in vain and feared lost forever. Mai was already famous for his discovery in 1815 of the works of Marcus Cornelius Fronto, and for his edition the following year of some fragments by Dionysius of Halicarnassus (both immediately studied and commented upon by Leopardi). He had been lavishly praised by Giordani in the *Biblioteca Italiana*; too lavishly in the opinion of Pietro Borsieri who, in his *Avventure letterarie d'un giorno* [Literary Adventures of One Day, 1816], said he preferred the achievements of original writers, both poets and scientists, and taunted Giordani with the following epigram:

Puro scrittor d'articoli
fai giganti i mezzani e grandi i piccoli,
e s'io chieggo: tal fallo emenderai?
tu mi torni a ripetere: Mai, mai!

[O writer of mere articles, you turn middling men into giants and small men into great ones; and if I ask you: Will you make amends? you keep replying: *Mai*, never!]

The limitations of Mai as a classical philologist are now well known, as they were to Leopardi who, in spite of his formally obsequious tone, was not a Mai-worshipper, had immediately rejected Mai's hypothesis on the origin of Dionysius's fragments, and had made several emendations to all the texts Mai edited, many of which the learned Monsignore later included in subsequent editions without ever giving Leopardi due credit. He even committed the unforgivable crime of publishing, as if he himself had discovered it, a text by Libanius which Leopardi had spotted among some codices in the Biblioteca Barberini and begun to study (1, 1160, 1168). The tone of the canzone is perfectly consonant with Leopardi's attitude to Mai, outwardly respectful but substantially independent of his influence. After a perfunctory celebration in the first three stanzas,

Mai's discoveries of the classics are soon left behind, and Leopardi moves on to a pregnant compendium of Italian cultural achievements (not exclusively literary, for he mentions Columbus). Their protagonists are characterized in a way reminiscent of Foscolo's references to great Italians in *I sepolcri*: Dante, Petrarch, Ariosto, Tasso and Alfieri stand out in Leopardi's canzone against the evils of their time, and point by implication to the evils of his own time which were far greater. Dante's hell is preferable to Italy, for there at least was justice. Petrarch's sorrows are better than present tedium and nothingness. Ariosto is described as the poet of illusions, and the words *nova speme d'Italia* (new hope of Italy, 111) ambiguously refer both to the poet and to the illusions he cherished. The envy from which Tasso suffered was preferable to the indifference surrounding great men in Leopardi's time. Nobody has followed Alfieri in waging war on the stage against tyrants. Every single reference to the past is matched in the poem by a pointed allusion to the present. Cicero, however, is never mentioned except in the title. The question arises: what is the connection between the discovery of *De Republica* and the contents of the poem?

It would seem that in 1820 there were reactionary and legitimist people who hoped that Cicero's book might lend support to their cause. Leopardi, however, with his superior knowledge of Cicero and of texts, such as St Augustine's *De civitate Dei* where the hitherto lost book had been summarized, knew such expectations to be false, as can be seen from the title of a political essay he intended to write (I, 370, 1). When in 1822 he was studying Mai's edition in a borrowed copy (Mai later presented him with one) he advised his father not to buy the book since it contained nothing that Cicero had not already said elsewhere: a singularly unconvincing reason considering Giacomo was then engaged in writing a masterly article on it that would attract the attention of no less a scholar than Barthold Niebuhr; but a sensible suggestion for someone like Monaldo who might have entertained false expectations about its contents. Like all other writers mentioned in the poem, Cicero was a pretext for a series of considerations affecting the social and political situation in Leopardi's time, which had very little to do with classical philology as practised by Mai and by Leopardi's contemporaries. Leopardi's idea that literature was only second best to action, was symbolized by the priority of *opra* (work) over *parola* (word) in line 41; the same idea was implied in the reference to Alfieri and openly expressed in the dedication of the poem to Count Leonardo

Trissino (see p.27). He later confirmed this in two of his *Operette morali* written in 1824, *Il Parini, ovvero della gloria* [Parini, or About Glory] and *Dialogo di Timandro e di Eleandro* [Dialogue of T. and E.]. Literature, Leopardi argued, has a very limited impact on its already few readers, and the only effect poetry can produce is at best a feeling of emotional purification lasting about half an hour. It is therefore difficult to believe what some critics, like Luigi Russo, suggest: that in this poem classical philology is seen as the spur to the moral and political regeneration of Italy. The informer of the Austrian police who had the poem banned was far more perceptive than many later critics.

Why was an innocent-looking canzone honouring a respected prelate branded as an ideologically subversive poem full of dread fanaticism? Restoration governments deliberately encouraged the intellectuals, often through high-level publications like *La biblioteca italiana*, to lapse into rhetoric as a substitute for action, and to transform the struggle between opposed social and political interests into a controversy between different literary theories. For a long time the real meaning of the Romantic controversy was disguised in this way. Leopardi, and any of his readers who happened to agree with him, could not be duped by such manoeuvres. *Ad Angelo Mai* plainly rejected the usual privileged notion of literature as the necessary inspiration for action, and therefore sapped the government's cultural policy. The poet must give up his exhortatory and inspirational postures. His real function is to put his readers to shame, to destroy their false expectations, to show them that illusions can console only if they are not mistaken for reality, to prove that all is vain except sorrow. In other words, he has to do what Dante, Petrarch, Ariosto, Tasso and Alfieri (according to Leopardi) did in their time. Barely a year after writing *Ad Angelo Mai*, at the end of a long and detailed essay in the *Zibaldone* on the relationship between language, literature and society (in which Fronto, another of Mai's discoveries, though criticised for being a purist, was praised for being far less backward-looking than contemporary Italian purists), Leopardi wrote:

> To put the Italian language back on its feet one should really begin by putting Italy back on its feet, and the Italians too, and refashion their hearts and minds; and the same should be said for literature...(*Zib.* 799)

One can now understand the absence from *Ad Angelo Mai* of any positive, optimistic encouragement. The heroic fantasy of *All'Italia* and the restrained but hopeful vision of the function of poetry in

Sopra il monumento di Dante are replaced in *Ad Angelo Mai* by complete and utter hopelessness:

> ...Io son distrutto
> né schermo alcuno ho dal dolor, ché scuro
> m'è l'avvenire, e tutto quanto io scerno
> è tal che sogno e fola
> fa parer la speranza... (ll.33–40)

[I am undone, and have no shield from sorrow, since the future is obscure to me, and whatever I discern is such as makes hope appear a dream and a fable.]

Between the composition of *Ad Angelo Mai* and the date of his departure for Rome on 17 November 1822 (he was to remain there just under six months) Leopardi wrote over half of his *Zibaldone*, began to sketch 'certain short satirical prose works' (Letter to Giordani, 4 Sept. 1820) that were later to develop into the *Operette morali*, and composed nine more poems. Two of them, *Nelle nozze della sorella Paolina* [On the Occasion of his Sister Paolina's Marriage] and *A un vincitore nel pallone* [To a Winner in the Game of Football], both written in 1821, complete the cycle of 'civic odes' begun with *All'Italia*. The hoped-for marriage of Paolina with Pier Andrea Peroli, which never took place (nor did any of her other matrimonial projects) and the athletic prowess of a certain Carlo Didimi were once more the pretext for Leopardi to write about what really mattered to him. In *Nelle nozze* Leopardi returned to the theme of woman's position in society: this time she is the sacrificial victim not of immorality and irresponsibility, like Virginia from Pesaro, but of honour and virtue, like the more famous Virginia mentioned in ancient Roman history. Love is not the cause of woman's downfall but the inspiration of lofty deeds; beauty turns woman not into an object of lust but into a source of virtuous emotions. 'Beauty is the natural companion of virtue' Leopardi had written in the *Zibaldone* shortly before (p. 1594). 'Beauty is usually joined to goodness' is the title he will later give to an excerpt from Castiglione's *Cortegiano* which he included in his *Crestomazia italiana (prosa)*. In many *Zibaldone* entries up to this time he had examined the connection between outward beauty and inner substance (which in men is actualized as virtue, and in objects as being functional to a purpose), and the correspondence between strength of body and mental vigour, with the consequent need for physical fitness (see Index to *Zibaldone* s.v. *corpo*). Being himself physically misshapen Leopardi was particulary sensitive to these issues, and *A un vincitore nel pallone* contains their imaginative and poetic development. It contains also structural features, typical words and motifs linking it to earlier (and later) *canti*: the complex network of assonances and rhythms of which we gave an example in the previous chapter; characteristic Leopardian expressions, like *forti errori, lieti inganni, le riposte faville* (reminiscent of *Sopra il monumento di Dante* l. 51 and *Ad Angelo Mai* l.60, and also of Foscolo's *Sepolcri* l. 118) and the themes of war and heroic sacrifice represented in previous poems by Thermopylae, the Russian campaign, the wars of Sparta, Marathon and, in the following poem *Bruto minore* [Brutus The Younger, December 1821] by the battle of Philippi. Connected with the evocation of heroic self-immolation are the idea that it is preferable to die than to live in a corrupt world, and the theme of suicide. Virginia willingly accepts death from her father's hands rather than yield to Appius Claudius's lust (*Nelle nozze*, ll. 76–90). The noble youth, champion in the game of football, should be loath to survive the ruin of his country, for life is only worth despising (*A un vincitore nel pallone*, ll. 53–60). In this way the idea of the acceptance of death merges with the contemplation of suicide, a theme touched upon in *La vita solitaria* [Solitary Life, 1821] and poetically developed in *Bruto minore* and *L'ultimo canto di Saffo* [Sappho's Last Song, May 1822].

Suicide was discussed very early in the *Zibaldone* where it first appeared (p. 40) as part of an unconvincing but ingenious proof of the immortality of the soul. The gist of it is that the human condition is inherently unhappy because man's nature makes him dissatisfied. But, since nature has given all other creatures an amount of happiness appropriate to their condition, it would be repugnant to her laws that man, the most perfect of all creatures should not have any. It follows that man's existence cannot be limited to its boundaries in time and space. Men who have no hope of a future life very reasonably kill themselves; and the very unnaturalness of the act, which runs counter to the principle of self-love, is evidence of their immortality. What is interesting in this argument is that it contains an admittedly contradictory notion of nature, taken as a value-free term in the case of man, but not in the case of the other creatures. Suicide is 'unnatural' in the value-loaded sense of 'nature'. This contradiction is further expounded in *Frammento sul suicidio* [Fragment on Suicide] probably written in this period, and in two passages of the *Zibaldone* (pp. 1978–82 of 23 Oct. 1821, and 2549–55 of July 1822). The second of those passages is sandwiched between two entries on physical beauty: one, written the previous day, saying

that what appears beautiful in a person, outside any aesthetic pre-
conception, is what reveals 'the disposition men have to life', in
other words, their inner vitality; the other, written a few days later,
saying that the lack of physical beauty is due to man's alienation
from his true nature. These entries give a new dimension both to the
celebration of Carlo Didimi's physical prowess, and to the inevitability of Sappho's suicide. Granted that man's life, according to
Leopardi's 'pleasure principle', is necessarily unhappy, the inevitable conclusion that *rationally* he should commit suicide is *not* an
argument in favour of suicide, but the ultimate proof of the des-
tructiveness of reason which alienates him from nature. The best
antidotes are the illusions both of imagination and of religion:
'wherever one meditates without imagination and enthusiasm one
comes to detest life; ... the knowledge of things brings about a death
wish' (*Frammento*, I, 199, I). The final message of *A un vincitore nel
pallone* is that a life unreasonably but generously and imaginatively
risked is a life gained. What matters is not the *act* of throwing one's
life away (an act Leopardi never attempted) but the *thought* of it,
which is the ultimate *reductio ad absurdum* of existence. This for
Leopardi is the real meaning of Marcus Brutus's suicide after Philippi,
which is the occasion in the poem for another scathing attack on the
'knowledge of things'. Brutus cannot survive his realization that
virtue is not a thing but a word (*Zib.* 523; Letter to Giordani of 26
April 1819; *Comparazione delle sentenze di Bruto minore e di Teofrasto
vicini a morte*, Comparison between the Last Words of Brutus the
Younger and Theophrastus). The poem is not so much about his
death, as about the end of antiquity, which from Leopardi's viewpoint was the youth of mankind, and was succeeded by 'the old age
of the world', that is, modern times:

> For we can say that the times of Brutus were the last age of the
> imagination, when science and the experience of truth finally
> prevailed, and what was enough to bring about the old age of
> the world became common knowledge. Otherwise he would
> not have had cause to flee from life as he did, nor would the
> Roman republic have died with him. Not only that, but the
> whole of antiquity, by which I mean the ancient characters and
> customs of all civilized nations were about to die, together with
> the beliefs that had produced and fostered them. (*Compara-
> zione*, I, 207, 2)

The most striking passages of *A un vincitore nel pallone* and *Bruto
minore* are in fact those visualizing the complete destruction of the

ancient civilization in an apocalyptic perspective of ruins inhabited by foxes and surveyed only by the silent white moon. They are directly prepared by *Zib.* 1 and 50, and by the final lines of *La sera del dì di festa* [The Evening of the Festive Day, 1820]:

> ... Or dov'è il suono
> di que' popoli antichi? or dov'è il grido
> de' nostri avi famosi, e il grande impero
> di quella Roma, e l'armi, e il fragorìo
> che n'andò per la terra e l'oceàno?
> Tutto è pace e silenzio, e tutto posa
> il mondo, e più di lor non si ragiona. (ll. 33–9)

[Where is now the sound of those ancient peoples? Where can the call be heard of our famous ancestors? and where is the great Roman empire with all its arms and clamour reaching throughout the land and the ocean? All is peace and silence, all the world is at rest, and they are no longer spoken about.]

Man's alienation from nature has both social and individual aspects. Brutus takes his life because of the way alienation affects the whole of mankind. The poet, in *La vita solitaria*, and his projection as Sappho contemplate suicide because of the way they see their personal relationship to nature, which appears warm at first, then neglectful (*La vita solitaria* ll. 14–23), finally totally indifferent (*Ultimo canto di Saffo*, ll. 23–7). In these and other poems (*Alla luna*, To the Moon, 1819 or 1820; *La sera del dì di festa* and *Bruto minore*, to mention only those of this period) the moon, invoked by the poet, seems to be the ambivalent symbol of nature, objectively cold and aloof but at the same time subjectively friendly and comforting (see also the letter to Giordani of 6 March 1820; I, 1094, 2). It is important to note this ambivalence because it accounts for the apparent 'development' and 'contradictoriness' of Leopardi's concept of nature: in this case too, as I already noted in respect of his earlier 'conversions' (p. 18 above), the evolutionary-chronological model must be handled with some caution. Furthermore the poet's realization of nature's attitude to men and his own emotional response to her are by no means identical. In *La sera del dì di festa* (ll. 14–16) Nature appears as actively hostile, and yet the poet's feelings towards her are warm. In the first of the four sections of *La vita solitaria* (ll. 1–22) he perceives nature as concerned only with the general happiness, and as being unmindful of the individual, but though he feels rejected he does not reject her. The remaining three sections (ll. 23–38, 39–69 and 70–107) are logically independent of

the first and of each other. They could all be read as separate idylls,
rehearsing themes and motifs of earlier and later poems (the countryside under the rain, silence and infinity, the fantasy and the reality of
love, the moon). And yet they share a common subject, aptly expressed by the title, which is the poet's loneliness, isolating him from
society, himself and love, but always reuniting him to nature.
Nature is 'holy', 'attractive' and has a motherly voice in *Alla primavera o delle favole antiche* [Spring, or about Ancient Fables,
January 1822]. The poet imagines her alive, and ready to speak to
men, and concerned with their fate, as she is presented in the
ancient fables. But this is an illusion, since nature is at best an im-
partial onlooker. And yet the poet, who no longer has trust in any
God and sees Fate as hostile, cannot help turning to Mother Nature
when he is dejected and despairing. Sappho did likewise. The Gods
and Fate denied her a share in the infinite beauty of creation, which is
personified by Nature, as an entity distinct from the Gods and Fate.
But for Leopardi this distinction cannot have any theoretical basis,
since Fate is what happens by the will of God, or the Gods, and
nature is everything there is; in fact as early as *Zibaldone* 393–4 he
had identified God and Nature. It has however an emotional basis
and a poetic function. The value-free notion of nature, as everything
there is and might also exist in an infinite number of other ways
(*Zib.* 1613–15), the indifferent and impersonal course of events,
destiny, can only be rationally apprehended by Leopardi. But he
also needs in his poetry a nature that is alive, sentient, endowed with
human attributes, whether responsive or aloof, benign or hostile,
mother or step-mother; not merely an abstract entity that he can
grasp in his philosophical speculations but a person he can speak and
relate to in his poems. The illusory quality of this dualistic vision of
nature is a poetic metaphor of the fact that nature is the greatest
provider of illusions, and that her benevolence (or, philosophically
speaking, the value-loaded concept of nature) is the greatest of her
illusions.

Alla Primavera was written shortly before the major outbreak in
1825 of the long-standing controversy over the use of mythology in
poetry. For orthodox classicists, mythology was an indispensable
formal adornment of the 'harsh truths' expressed by poetry. For
romantic theorists it was a ready-made set of images no longer suited
to the modern age: they were however unable to suggest a viable
alternative and mostly contented themselves with replacing one set of
clichés with another. Leopardi clearly saw, as we have already noted

(p. 23ff.) that no myths, or popular errors, or illusions of any kind were valuable to the poet unless his own imagination had fashioned them by listening to the voice of nature. Classical myths were poetic only insofar as they had been created by men not yet alienated from nature, and therefore enshrined for all times basic imaginative archetypes relevant to all men. Classical mythology in the 1820s was about to die not because it had been replaced by new romantic myths, but because mythopoetic imagination had become subservient either to a sterile tradition or to an empty ideology of progress.

So, apart from a few poignant hints in *Alla Primavera*, Leopardi did not make use of classical mythology in his *Canti*. He began by drawing inspiration from the facts of political and cultural history in his 'civic odes', and continued by writing poetry about the illusions which nature builds up and human reason destroys.

7. 'A Touch of Irony'

On 17 November 1822 two coaches left Recanati taking Marquis Carlo Antici, his family and his brother Don Girolamo, who had spent the summer in their home town, back to Rome. On this occasion Monaldo relented and let Giacomo accompany them. The journey took about a week and Giacomo found it passably enjoyable, though supremely uncomfortable. Having arrived in Rome, however, he fell prey to a feeling of utter bewilderment. He felt he had totally lost his bearings, 'wholly alone and naked in the midst of my relatives', as he put it in his first letter to Carlo. His subsequent letters, totally uninhibited to Carlo and Paolina, rather more cautious to Monaldo, show that the long hoped-for escape from Recanati had turned into a great disappointment. He found his hosts noisy and selfish, their household a shambles, the most notable intellectuals, with a few exceptions, complete nonentities. Roman society appeared to him frivolous and corrupt. Women of all classes he thought disgusting: of high-class courtesans he could not speak because he had not met any, but ordinary whores were much nicer in Recanati. The very scale of Rome's fabrics seemed to him out of all human proportion: 'those huge buildings and those consequently interminable streets are so many spaces thrown in between men, instead of being spaces containing men' (1, 1131, 2). The only street he liked was in a working-class district he walked through on his way to Tasso's tomb:

> It is bordered throughout its length by workshops, and is full of the noise of looms and other instruments, and of the songs of working men and women. In an idle, dissolute, disorganized town, as capitals are, it is beautiful to contemplate a picture of collected and well-ordered life, engaged in useful occupations. Even the features and manners of people one comes across in that street are somewhat more genuine and humane than elsewhere, and show the customs and characters of people whose life is founded on truth and not on falsehood; who live by their work and not by intrigue, imposture and deceit, like the greater part of that population. (1, 1150, 2)

Most critics quoting this letter pay attention only to Leopardi's emotions while visiting Tasso's grave, 'the first and only pleasure' he had had in Rome up to that moment. And yet his description of a working-class street so much more human and lively than the empty scenography of monumental Rome is just as important as evidence of Leopardi's constant concern with the social (not merely the moral) significance of work, and the social responsibility of those who depend on other people's work. Unlike all those who, throughout the nineteenth century, identified the working classes with the 'dangerous' and delinquent classes, Leopardi declared in 1820 that 'rampant misconduct is found only among the idle classes' (*Zib.*131). He believed happiness could be found in work (*Zib.*172–3). He thought it useless to preach morality to a badly governed people: practical morality depended upon the nature of social institutions (see p.110). And social institutions, obliging as they did a large part of mankind to work in harmful and insanitary conditions, to produce luxury goods such as precious metals, sugar or coffee, or to live in slavery, were barbarous, uncivilized and unnatural (*Zib.* 870–1, 1170–3). When reading in the *Canti* about the farm labourer (*Alla sua donna* 35), the servants in the Leopardi household (*Le ricordanze* 18–19), the artisan, the cart driver (*La quiete dopo la tempesta* 11, 23), the old woman spinning with her neighbours, the whistling peasant, the carpenter (*Il sabato del villaggio* 9, 29, 34) one must remember that for Leopardi they were not ornamental figures, like the Arcadian shepherds, but real working people such as he knew and loved. The community of feelings and hopes that he imagined could exist between himself and a working girl like his coachman's daughter Teresa Fattorini, transfigured as Silvia, is symbolized in the poem *A Silvia* by the fact that they are both working at the same time, the poet at his books, the girl at her loom.

Work, not merely his beloved literary studies but the kind that gives a man dignity and allows him to support himself, was something Leopardi needed very badly, if he wanted to become financially (and emotionally) independent of his family. While he was in Rome, the publisher Mariano De Romanis asked him to undertake a translation of Plato's complete works. His uncle, Carlo Antici, encouraged him to accept, because he thought it would remove from his nephew the stigma of unorthodoxy, but Monaldo was against the idea. He considered it demeaning for Giacomo to work for a publisher who, according to his calculations would pay his son little more than he gave the family cook; but at the same time he was not prepared to

give Giacomo a regular and dependable allowance at least as good as
the cook's wages. In the end nothing came of the De Romanis's
project. Later, however, Leopardi worked for a period of several
years, in an advisory and editorial capacity, for the Milanese publisher Antonio Fortunato Stella, with whom he had been in contact
since 1816. Another possible source of income for Giacomo could
have been teaching; but because of his shyness and ill health he considered himself unfit for academic work, and he found private
tuition mentally unrewarding and physically taxing. Before going to
Rome he had applied to Mai for a post in the Vatican Library, which
he thought carried some sort of academic status: it turned out to be
a copyist job which had anyway already been promised to someone
else. When, a few years later, two offers of teaching jobs came his
way, he could not, or was not prepared to accept them.

The best form of employment for Leopardi would have been
some sort of Government sinecure giving him a modicum of
financial security and plenty of free time to do what he really
wanted. Nearly all civil service careers in the Papal administration,
however, had various strings attached, and many carried only a
token salary. Leopardi did not like any offer or opportunity that
carried duties or obligations conflicting with his idea of personal
freedom. He therefore consistently refused not only to enter Holy
Orders but also to wear any kind of religious habit or uniform. That
made it practically impossible for him to be employed in the Papal
civil service, or to be given some ecclesiastical benefice which was a
prerogative of his family. At one time it seemed that one of the
friends he had made in Rome, the classical historian Barthold Georg
Niebuhr, who was then Prussian ambassador to the Vatican and had
realized the young poet's exceptional gifts, would be successful in
persuading Cardinal Consalvi, the Secretary of State, to appoint
Leopardi as Tax Inspector; but then the Pope died, Cardinal Consalvi
lost his Secretaryship, and Leopardi's application fell into abeyance.
At the end of April 1823 the poet left Rome without having been
able to find there the sort of work that would have freed him from
the need to return to Recanati. Back home, he continued to write to
the Cardinal, and to Niebuhr and his first secretary Karl von
Bunsen, hoping that something might still be done in his favour; but
it became increasingly clear that he was *persona non grata*. In December 1823 he sent Brighenti the manuscript of nine of his poems to
which he had added a new canzone, *Alla sua donna*, written two
months earlier. Brighenti was to have them published in Bologna,

but he met with the censor's opposition: twice they refused to grant the necessary licence on the grounds that the poems contained things that offended the Monarchs and slighted Virtue. When finally the poems were permitted to be published in 1824, they were used as evidence against Leopardi, who as a consequence lost the post of Secretary of the Fine Arts Academy in Bologna, which he had almost been promised through the good offices of Bunsen (then Niebuhr's successor). That put an end to Leopardi's hopes of becoming financially independent.

Alla sua donna is reminiscent of two earlier love poems, *Il primo amore* and *Il sogno*, which have been interpreted by commentators as expressions of idealized or 'Platonic' love. The former was Leopardi's first love poem, written in 1817 soon after the visit of a distant relative, 26-year-old Gertrude Cassi Lazzeri. In his *Diario del primo amore* young Giacomo left a description of her suggesting that he felt a strong physical attraction for her. She had prominent but pleasing features and was taller and bigger than any woman he had ever seen ('alta e membruta quanto nessuna donna ch'io m'abbia veduta mai', I, 353, 1): her physical type was one by which Giacomo felt particularly subjugated (I, 355, 1). Gertrude probably never suspected that her young cousin had towards her any feelings worth reciprocating, and, in this sense he 'burned with a pure unsullied fire'. But shapely Gertrude was no Platonic idea. The adjective *torbido* (turbid, sullied) is twice used by Leopardi with reference to his emotions in his *Diario*. In the poem Leopardi used Petrarchan and Bembian vocabulary because it was the only one available to him; but there is no mistaking the sensual intensity of expressions like 'M'affaticavi in su le piume il fianco/ad ogni or fortemente palpitando' [you, my heart, belaboured my breast, as I was lying in bed, with strong frequent throbs]. Of course expressions such as those were conventional, but they were considered as conventionally appropriate to the poetic symbolization of sexual emotions. It would be wrong to imply that, because the poetic symbols were chaste, the emotions were also chaste; or that, because the symbols are conventional, the emotions were so too (see also pp. 102–3). *Il sogno*, which should be connected with the notes *Del fingere poetando un sogno* [How to Describe a Dream in Poetry, I, 349] written in December 1820, gives a picture of ideal love not because of any idea of purity, or any sublimation of sexual emotions, but simply because the poet's beloved is necessarily reduced to the status of idea as a consequence of her untimely death. The poem in fact is not so much about love as about the theme, dear to Leopardi, of the death of young people, which to him seemed one of the greatest cruelties of nature. If *Il sogno* was about a no-longer existent woman, *Alla sua donna* was about a non-existent woman, 'a woman such as cannot be found'. In a facetious note appended to the nine poems sent to Brighenti, Leopardi made the point that none of their titles had anything to do with their real subject: there was no mention in them of codices, marriage, football or the countryside in Spring. Similarly *Alla sua donna* was not about 'his' woman, or indeed about any real woman. Following from the Platonizing interpretations of the previous two love poems, some commentators have suggested that in *Alla sua donna* woman is presented as a Platonic idea. To support this view *Zibaldone* 1712–14 is often quoted out of context, as if Leopardi intended to praise Plato's 'system of ideas pre-existing to things', and his canzoni were consequently a celebration of Platonic love. What Leopardi in fact meant was totally different (see also *Zib.* 351, 1342, 2709). Given men's inclination to believe in the absolute (which he rejected) he held that Plato's hypothesis concerning ideas as models was admirably ingenious as a justification of such a false belief; but he concluded that it was amazing that men could reject Plato's hypothesis on ideas as being false and inconsistent while holding on to their belief in the absolute. Far from being an argument in favour of Platonism those pages from the *Zibaldone* were a plea for philosophical relativism. In view of Leopardi's well-documented aversion from Platonism his reference to Plato's eternal ideas must have a decidedly sceptical flavour. Indeed the whole canzone makes more sense if, following the lead given by the poet himself in his *Annotazioni* (1, 56–7), one takes it not as a serious celebration of ideal womanhood but as an ironical comment on the ease with which men mistakenly turn the illusions of love into emotional realities.

A few days before writing *Alla sua donna* Leopardi had argued in his *Zibaldone* (3302–10) that all the seemingly spiritual ideas and emotions men have when in love are nothing but muddled thoughts and false beliefs, owing to society having departed from the ways of nature and to the disguising effects of civilization and fashion, which prevented women from appearing as they really are. In their natural state women would be naked, and would arouse straight-forwardly sexual desires. In our civilized society they are clothed, and arouse displaced, confused, idealized, complicated emotions, inducing men falsely to deify them and to imagine them almost as if they belonged to a different species. This argument is an uncompromising rejection of Platonic love.

About the same time Leopardi wrote a letter to the Belgian writer A. M. Jacopssen whom he had met in Rome. In this letter, which commentators frequently quote in connection with the poem, Leopardi confessed that often an imagined love object appeared to him preferable to a real one; but he made this point in the context of a series of reflections on the despair he felt when facing reality and discovering that the illusions are the only real and socially valuable thing. 'Le bonheur de l'homme ne peut consister dans ce qui est réel', Leopardi wrote (Man's happiness cannot consist in what is real). Should one then believe that it lies in the ideal? It would be a wise thing to do, if one could bring oneself to believe it; but Leopardi could not:

> C'est la véritable sagesse que de chercher ce bonheur dans l'idéal, comme vous faites. Pour moi je regrette le temps où il m'était permis de l'y chercher, et je vois avec une sorte d'effroi que mon imagination devient stérile et me refuse tous les secours qu'elle me prêtait autrefois. [It is really wise to look to the ideal for happiness, as you do. For myself, I regret the time when it was possible for me to do so, and see with a sort of terror that my imagination is becoming sterile and refuses to help me as it did in the past.] (I, 1166, 2)

It is easy to draw the conclusion that, if Leopardi did not find happiness in reality and could not find it in the ideal, he believed it was nowhere to be found; and to take this as evidence of his irredeemable pessimism. But it would be a misleading conclusion. The point is that man cannot find happiness in the ideal because he has a wrong conception of it. No man, Leopardi believed, has ever been able to imagine the ideal without attributing to it some sort of sensual reality (*Zib.* 1388–91); and since all human experience is material and sensual and all human faculties are material and matter-bound man naturally imagines the spirit as some sort of impalpable and disembodied matter, but still as matter nevertheless (*Zib.* 601, 1026, 1262). 'The heart may well imagine it loves the spirit or feels something immaterial, but it is absolutely mistaken' (*Zib.* 1694). The problem is that the necessary terminological distinction between matter and spirit, which Leopardi also accepts (*Zib.* 1635–6), seems to entail the existence of some sort of spiritual reality separate from material reality. But how should one conceive of that 'existence'? To believe that our use of words necessarily implies the 'existence' of the separate realities named by those words would be a crude form of ontological realism. Leopardi's solution, though scattered through various pages of the *Zibaldone*, is fairly clear. All our mental faculties can form immaterial concepts only if we reduce them to matter, that is, to words, for language is the materialization process of abstract ideas (*Zib.* 1657–8). Granted that there should be a terminological distinction between reality (or matter) and the thought that conceives it, the spirit is *not* a part, however indefinite, disembodied or impalpable, of the reality which is the object of thought, but is part of thought itself, embodied in words; and words are the body, not the envelope, of thought (*Zib.* 1694). What men usually call 'spirit' is inevitably, and mistakenly, projected *outside* thought, into matter itself. This kind of spiritualism is a dangerous folly (*Zib.* 4208). 'Our intellect is the only place where time, space, and many other abstract things, have independent existence in themselves, and are something' (*Zib.* 4233). It follows implicitly that the consoling illusions cannot draw their strength from being part of an alleged spiritual reality existing outside human thought. Their reality can only be of a conceptual nature. Illusions are not symbols of unrealized facts, pointers to hopeful possibilities, signs of anything real. They cannot be embodied into something else. Their only body is the words expressing them. The only body of 'the woman who cannot be found' either in the golden age, or on earth, or among Platonic ideas, or on some other world in space, is Leopardi's poem. The only possible destiny for an apostle of illusions like Leopardi was to be a writer of words.

The delicately ironical tone of *Alla sua donna* is also evident in the abundance—in the short space of 55 lines of verse—of stylistic features typical of Leopardi in his sceptical or sarcastic mood (eight conditional clauses introduced by *se* or *o*, with two more conditional verbs, and one dubitative clause preceded by *forse*). The poem was composed shortly before the period when Leopardi occupied himself almost entirely in developing the 'short satirical prose-works' he had begun in 1820 (see p.48 above) into the *Operette morali* [Short Moral Treatises; Leopardi's own 'English' translation was 'Moral Performances' 1, 1269, 1]. Between January and November 1824 he wrote twenty-one of them and, probably in March, he drafted a *Discorso sopra lo stato presente dei costumi degli italiani* [Discourse on the Present State of Italian Society] which he left unfinished, but which is an important and acute diagnosis of the ills afflicting his country. He himself described his undertaking, attributing it to

Socrates, in *Detti memorabili di Filippo Ottonieri* [Memorable Sayings by F.O.]:

> Born with a most gentle nature, therefore greatly inclined to love, but with an exceedingly ill-shaped body,...poor, un-loved, ill suited to the intrigues of public life, and nevertheless gifted with a great mind, which must have disproportionately increased the vexations caused by his state, he began, as an idle pursuit, to reason shrewdly about the actions, customs and qualities of his fellow-citizens, in which pursuit he displayed a touch of irony, as it beseemed a man who, so to speak, was prevented from having a share in life. But the gentleness and magnanimity of his nature...caused his irony to be not bitter and biting but mellow and mild. (i, 137–8)

After *Alla sua donna* Leopardi spent over four years without writing poetry, if one excepts *Epistola al conte Carlo Pepoli* [Epistle to Count C.P., March 1826], which is no great poem, but a dignified and elegant dissertation on the theme of the futility of work when it is not conducive to human happiness, and the dreary emptiness of leisure for those who can afford not to work but are unable to fill their life with worthy occupations. The programme Leopardi had chosen for himself was outlined in ll. 140–8:

> ...L'acerbo vero, i ciechi
> destini investigar delle mortali
> e dell'eterne cose; a che prodotta
> a che d'affanni e di miserie carca
> l'umana stirpe; a quale ultimo intento
> lei spinga il fato e la natura; a cui
> tanto nostro dolor diletti o giovi:
> con quali ordini e leggi a che si volva
> questo arcano universo...
> [To investigate the bitter truth, the blind destiny of mortal and eternal things; what mankind was created for, and why it is laden with anguish and misery; towards what end Fate and Nature lead it, who receives benefit or pleasure from our sorrows; by what orders or laws this mysterious universe is ruled and to what purpose.]

By the end of 1823 this programme was nearly complete. Leopardi's investigations already filled 4007 out of 4527 pages of his *Zibaldone*. The *Zibaldone* was a personal repository of ideas, a private intellectual tool; and its arguments, relentlessly spiralling forward through repetitions and developments of previous observations, full

of cross-references and notes, were not in a form suitable for public
use. And yet it is evident that Leopardi did not intend to keep his
'bitter truths' to himself. In *Zib.* 1720, for instance, he appeared
concerned with their reception by the general public; and the aside
on page 2056 ('I don't know whether the interpretation I give of
this passage is true...It's enough for me that it explains my thought
to myself') seems intended to justify a possible mistake in the eyes
of an imaginary reader. After 1832 he collected for publication 111
Pensieri, 71 of which are paraphrases of passages from pages of the
Zibaldone. The question of how Leopardi's ideas would be received
by the public appears again at the end of the *Epistola*:

> ...E se del vero
> ragionando talor sieno alle genti
> o mal grati i miei detti o non intesi
> non mi dorrò, che già del tutto il vago
> desio di gloria antico in me fia spento.

> [And if people will reject or misunderstand what I say when I
> reason about the truth, I shall not complain, because the old
> desire for glory is altogether extinguished in me.]

Leopardi had been considering for some time the question how to
develop a good Italian prose style. He often discussed this with
Giordani, from the very early stages of their correspondence. In a
letter to Giordani dated 13 July 1821, he wrote:

> He who wants to serve Italy well must above all show her a
> philosophical language, without which I believe she will never
> have a modern literature of her own, and not having a modern
> literature of her own will never become a nation. (1, 1123, 1)

It seems from this letter that Leopardi's earlier idea, of the unity
between true philosophy and poetry (see p. 30 above) had developed
into the idea of combining scientific thought and literary craftmanship into a language the Italian nation needed for her intellectual and
social development. It should of course be remembered that the
term *filosofia* in Leopardi's time still included what we would call
to-day 'scientific knowledge'. Leopardi included among the 'scientists' not only physicists and mathematicians who, in his opinion,
had no hope of attaining literary perfection, indeed had little or no
use for it, but also moralists, political scientists, psychologists, meta-
physicians and philosophers *stricto sensu*, who had some chance of
achieving it (*Zib.* 2725–31). In order to elaborate his new philosophical language Leopardi had studied with particular attention the
writings of Italian scientists, such as Galileo Galilei; his disciple

Vincenzo Viviani; Lorenzo Magalotti, disciple of Viviani and Malpighi; the biologist Francesco Redi, who was the first to disprove the legend of the spontaneous generation of insects; Francesco Algarotti, popularizer of Newtonian physics; the astronomer Eustachio Zanotti; the physicist Francesco Maria Zanotti, author of a famous treatise on 'live force' (i.e. kinetic energy); and his disciple, the mathematician Luigi Palcani; to mention only those Leopardi included in his 1827 anthology of Italian prose-writers.

And yet, in their studies on the *Operette morali*, critics have often disregarded Leopardi's deliberate intention of combining scientific rigour with literary craftmanship, and the ideological significance of the work as a statement of its author's scientific outlook. As a consequence the *Operette morali* have been found wanting according to those very criteria of formal, 'geometrical' philosophy Leopardi had declaredly rejected as incompatible with poetry (see p. 30 above). Poetry has been considered as a fragmentary, if welcome, intrusion into his abstract reasoning; and *operette* to which Leopardi attached great importance, such as the *Frammento apocrifo di Stratone da Lampsaco*, a glorification of materialistic cosmology, or the *Dialogo di Timandro e di Eleandro* which is a sort of preface to the whole work (Leopardi's letter to Stella of 16 June 1826) have been summarily dismissed as 'of little significance' (Fubini) or as 'alien to Leopardi's true nature' (Menotti Ciardo). On the whole Leopardi was a good prophet when he forecast, in the first public presentation of his 'bitter truths', that people would reject or misunderstand what he had to say.

8. Pessimism or Anti-optimism

During the fifteen months Leopardi spent in Recanati after his return from Rome, he persevered in his attempts to secure some sort of paid employment that would enable him to gain a measure of financial independence from his family, and leave home again (see pp. 55–6 above). In the Spring of 1825 the Milanese publisher Antonio Fortunato Stella asked Leopardi's opinion on a project by an unnamed scholar for a complete edition of Cicero's works. Leopardi's report, a model of its kind, full of extremely wise and sound methodological remarks on how the edition of a classic should be undertaken (I, 1199–1200), was politely unfavourable: and that may well be one of the reasons why the unnamed scholar—who was none other than Niccolò Tommaseo—began to hate him. Stella, greatly impressed, decided to drop Tommaseo and entrust the edition to Leopardi, whom he invited to spend some time in Milan as his guest. Leopardi accepted, obtained a passport (this time with his father's consent, as he pointedly stated in his application), and left towards the middle of July 1825. This was the beginning of a business association with Stella that lasted until the end of 1828, and resulted in the publication of a commentary to Petrarch's *Rime* (1826), two anthologies of Italian prose (1827) and poetry (1828) and the *Operette morali* (1827). A first sample of the latter (three dialogues: *Dialogo di Timandro e di Eleandro*, *Dialogo di Cristoforo Colombo e di Pietro Gutierrez* and *Dialogo di Torquato Tasso e del suo genio familiare*) appeared in 1826 in the Florentine periodical *Antologia*. Its editor, Giampietro Vieusseux, was a Swiss businessman who had settled in Florence in 1818 and had become one of the most prominent and praiseworthy cultural organizers in nineteenth-century Italy. In 1824 he had invited Leopardi to write for the *Antologia* regular reviews and contributions on literary and scientific matters in the States of the Church, but Leopardi had declined to accept. He doubted whether there was any intellectual life worth writing about in the States of the Church, and from such as there was he felt completely cut off. He thought moreover that a periodical like Vieusseux's, the first one worthy of the Italian name, 'ought rather to teach what should be done than to inform about what is being done', and he would have preferred to write not merely reports and reviews but original articles 'of a philosophical nature'. (I, 1179–80). He therefore gave Vieusseux the three dialogues to publish, but was rather disappointed when they appeared 'with many and terrible misprints, and barbarous spelling' (I, 1242, I). Leopardi was perhaps more attached to the *Operette morali* than to any other of his works. He told Stella that he would rather lose his head than its manuscript (I, 1251–2); and he did not take at all to Stella's idea that the work should first appear by instalments in the Milanese journal *Nuovo Ricoglitore*, or that it should be published as a pocket book in a series called 'Amusing and Educational Books for Gentlewomen' (I, 1274). When the *Operette* finally appeared they were not well received, and they were completely overshadowed by 'Manzoni's Christian novel' (I, 1316, I), about which Leopardi's views were not as favourable as it has often been alleged (I, 1316, I; 1292, I). The two writers met in Florence in 1827, where Leopardi had repaired after a short spell in Milan, as Stella's guest, and a long period of residence in Bologna (September 1825–June 1827: but he spent the winter 1826–7 at home). They were too profoundly different in outlook to make any significant contact. Leopardi's last recorded reference to Manzoni appears in the famous letter to Monaldo to justify his public disclaim of the authorship of Monaldo's *Dialoghetti*, in which he said that he would have similarly disclaimed the authorship of *I promessi sposi* had the novel been attributed to him (I, 1383, 2). The reference might have appeared flattering to Monaldo, who of course loved Manzoni; but knowing that Giacomo considered his father's book infamous, evil, fanatical and filthy (I, 1381, I), it seems hardly flattering to Manzoni. On his part, Manzoni later in life confessed to Francesco De Sanctis that he 'could not understand how Leopardi could pass as a poet'.

By December 1828 Stella's remittance, which up to then had allowed Leopardi to eke out a precarious living in Bologna, Florence and Pisa, had finally stopped. Leopardi was wintering in Recanati, for the last time, and desperately needed to escape again, but he lacked the means to do so. His friends in Bologna and Florence were trying their best to find him some employment. Giacomo Tommasini, a famous doctor, professor of physiology and pathology at Bologna University, whose wife and daughter were among the best friends Leopardi ever had, tried, through his son-in-law Ferdinando Maestri, to obtain a teaching job for Leopardi in

Parma, and in January 1829 Maestri wrote offering him the Chair of
Natural History at Parma University (not certainly the subject
Leopardi was most interested in, but not an entirely unlikely choice,
considering the extent and depth of Leopardi's scientific interests).
This offer, however, was not confirmed, and Leopardi was never too
keen to accept it. A way out of his financial difficulties would have
been for him to win the thousand *scudi* literary prize to be awarded
in 1830 by the Accademia della Crusca in Florence. He entered the
Operette morali, but soon formed the impression that the judges were
not in his favour, and that they would rather give the prize to *I
promessi sposi* (which had not been entered) than to the *Operette*.
Only one vote was given to Leopardi's book (nearly all the others
going to Botta's 'History of Italy from 1789 to 1814') and the final
report by Gino Capponi expressed the regret that *I promessi sposi*
could not be given an unofficial prize.

It is not difficult to see why the *Operette morali* failed to please.
Under the paternalistic and tolerably enlightened rule of Leopold II,
Tuscan intellectuals, particularly those gathering round Capponi and
Vieusseux, were full of optimism and saw themselves as the true
intermediaries between the rulers and the people. Vieusseux was so
much persuaded that his review was the best instrument of communication between the government and the governed (a communication
which, in his mind, was the next best thing to constitutional rule)
that he failed to understand why the *Antologia* was repeatedly
hounded by official censorship, and finally suppressed in 1833. In a
review of Monti's *Sermone sulla Mitologia* (Discourse on Mythology), published in the *Antologia* in October 1825, Giuseppe
Montani, a former collaborator of *Il conciliatore* and a correspondent
of Leopardi (p.24), painted a portrait of the progressive Romantic
intellectual as he, and no doubt his friends, imagined him: looking at
the most important factories and shops of his town and pledging his
pen to the support of the industrial revolution; contemplating, from
one of the wharves in the harbour, all the ships flying their various
national flags, symbols of international brotherhood; paying homage
to the genius of George Canning and James Watt, creators respectively of free trade and of the steam engine. The anti-optimistic
argument of the *Operette*, with its insistence that man is puny and
irrelevant to the general scheme of creation, that this is not the best
of all possible worlds, that individual happiness is more important
than so-called social progress; also with its uncompromising rejection of all mendacious consolations of idealism, spiritualism and

religion, together with its confutation of the beliefs in human perfectibility and the providential order of things, ran completely counter to the beliefs of the Tuscan intellectuals. While they were prepared to do their best to support Leopardi and to help him, deep down they could not forgive him. When, in 1835, Leopardi once more satirized their beliefs, in a pretended recantation to Gino Capponi, Capponi defined him, in a letter to Vieusseux, 'that accursed hunchback, who is trying to take the piss out of me'.

On his part, though recognizing the importance of Vieusseux's periodical while it lasted, Leopardi was out of sympathy with its methods. 'We are in the century of moral, economic and political sciences, and of natural and mathematical sciences' proclaimed the *Antologia*. But Leopardi, writing in 1828 to Giordani, commented:

> 'I can't get it into my head that the highest achievement of human knowledge consists in knowing politics and statistics... Thus it happens that what is pleasurable seems to me far more useful than all the useful things, and literature truly and positively more useful than all those dry sciences, which, even if they achieved their ends, would do very little for the real happiness of men, who are individuals and not people. But when are they actually going to achieve those ends? I should like one of our professors of historical sciences to tell me'.
> (I, 1321, I)

Words that sound like an implied criticism of the *Antologia*'s editorial line can also be found in the programme for a new periodical, *Lo Spettatore Fiorentino*, which Leopardi proposed to edit in 1832 (I, 992–3). The project, which might have assured Leopardi a small income, fell through because of governmental opposition. Giacomo had been classified as ideologically suspect by the Florentine police.

He was, of course, neither against science nor against technological and social progress. In an entry in the *Zibaldone* (4185–8) which he significantly summarized in his own index under the heading *Felicità* (Happiness), he declared himself 'directly and fundamentally favourable' to the activity and energy pervading Europe in his own time, and to 'civilization considered as increasing occupation, movement, real life, action, and providing the means thereof'. But he was against the ideological mystification of progress, and consequently distrusted what he called 'historical' and we would call social sciences, over which the *Antologia* enthused; and this explains why he, who had shown himself in his *Discorso sopra lo stato presente dei costumi degli italiani*, an extremely acute and perceptive observer of society, affected, in writing to Vieusseux, complete ignorance of social philosophy (1, 1243, 1). He was very much interested in such marvels of contemporary technology as pressure cookers (*La scommessa di Prometeo*), robots, lightning conductors (*Proposta di premi fatta all'Accademia dei Sillografi*), not to mention the telegraph, aircraft and steam engines (*Zib.* 4198–9). He knew about the dietetic studies of Christoph Wilhelm Hufeland, whose memory survives today in the term *macrobiotics*, which he was the first to popularize (*Makrobiotik, oder die Kunst das menschliche Leben zu verlängern*, Jena, 1798; referred to in *Dialogo di un Fisico e di un metafisico*). But he did not consider technological progress as essential to a happy life, and thought that a happy life was preferable to one artificially prolonged by medical science. Perhaps because of his own ailing health, which medical science of his time was unable to improve, Leopardi knew many doctors, but did not have a high opinion of their art (*Zib.* 1338). In a letter to Vieusseux of 21 January 1832 (1, 1373–4), he recommended some of them as possible scientific correspondents to the *Antologia*: Domenico Morichini, well-known for his studies on the therapeutic effects of mineral waters; Giuseppe de Matthaeis, who was also a noted antiquarian; Vincenzo Valorani, who taught 'practical medicine' at Bologna University, and was also author of translations from Greek poets; Michele Medici, who held the Chair of Physiology at Bologna, and was later to write a historical memoir on the scientific and literary academics of that town; and Francesco Puccinotti, whom Leopardi had known and corresponded with since 1825, having consulted him on the subject of Ruysch and his mummies at the time of the composition of the *Operette*. He also mentioned in the same letter Count Domenico Paoli, author of a substantial treatise on molecular motion in solid bodies, which he had read (*Zib.* 4242) probably because of the large amount of information it contained on geological changes; Marquess Petrucci, 'a good scientist' and an unnamed Professor of Physics at Ravenna. Doctors at the time occupied a particular cultural position, halfway between the moral and natural sciences, and had a traditional inclination towards literary studies. This made them eminently suited to Vieusseux's editorial programme, even if *L'Antologia* excluded specifically medical articles as a matter of policy.

Leopardi disliked the so-called exact sciences because they were not conducive to literature (see p. 62), and also because they led him away from nature: since the real causal relationships are so infinite and complicated as to be practically unknowable, physics and mathematics (not unlike the physiology and chemistry of his time, in that respect) had to resort to fictitious generalizations, such as absolute vacuum, perfectly smooth and hard bodies, etc., (*Zib.* 3977–8), and ended by resembling metaphysics (*Zib.* 4302–4). Leopardi preferred the natural sciences to the exact sciences, as the former are less amenable to idealistic and metaphysical interpretations: that is astronomy (which he had studied since childhood), geology, paleontology and geography, which, between the eighteenth and the nineteenth century had been in the forefront of the fight against theological, teleological, spiritualistic and anti-historical interpretations of nature. References to these sciences abound in the *Operette morali*. There is mention of the recently confirmed flattening of the Earth at the poles, of continental drift (*Dialogo d'Ercole e d'Atlante*), of the latest astronomical observations of Gruithuisen, Schröter and Herschel (*Dialogo della terra e della luna*), of the discovery of fossils (*Dialogo di un folletto e gnomo*), and of materialistic cosmological theories (*Frammento apocrifo di Stratone da Lampsaco*). Leopardi preferred these sciences, the methodology of which transcended mere mathematico-geometrical processes of induction in order to achieve an imaginative awareness of the system of relations between things in nature. This scientific methodology is what transformed dry academic philosophy into the kind of superphilosophy that he needed to be a poet (p. 31). But poetry for him was also a method for the investigation of nature, since 'nature and all universal things are composed, conformed and ordained to a poetic effect' (*Zib.* 3241).

Nature, as the study of geology and paleontology had taught Leopardi and some of his contemporaries, has absolute priority over man, who appeared on this earth very late in the history of the world. Nature dwarfs and dominates him. Whatever he may believe about his providential destiny and his privileged position in the 'great chain of beings', man is ultimately irrelevant to nature's scheme of things. The Newtonian cosmic machine would work just as well without him, and does not work for his benefit. This might superficially appear an argument tending to reduce man's dignity and to displace him from the centre of philosophical concern—but it is not so. For it is precisely man's irrelevance in a cosmos where everything appears to have a purpose and a fitness for that purpose that raises the question—what is man for? Why is man so imperfect and weak? Why is he inevitably unhappy? And it is precisely by his ability to ask himself such questions that man achieves the highest possible intellectual power and moral dignity (*Zib.* 3171–2). A materialistic and truly scientific world-view must necessarily end by concerning itself most closely with man's situation, and basically with the problem of his well-being and happiness, which, as Timpanaro rightly remarked, was in the eighteenth and nineteenth centuries a truly scientific problem (one has only to think of all the innumerable treatises on happiness and pleasure written in that period). This is the link between science and ethics, which may explain why a work in which Leopardi condensed the essence of his materialistic thought and scientific culture, was not called by him *Operette scientifiche* but *Operette morali*. He insisted that the scientific (*materiale*) investigation of nature should extend also to the moral sphere (*Zib.* 3241).

Eleander, the author's mouthpiece, in *Dialogo di Timandro e di Eleandro*, thus sums up the message of the *Operette*:

> I desire as much as you do, and as much as anyone else, the well-being of my species in all things; but I have no hope for it. I cannot rejoice and put my trust in certain good expectations, like many philosophers in this century. My hopelessness, being absolute, continual, founded on a firm judgement and on certainty, does not allow me to indulge in dreams and happy imaginations for the future, nor to embark on any enterprise in order to bring them to fruition. (1, 164, 1)

Does this uncompromising rejection of optimism amount to pessimism? Looking at this question from a purely logical point of view I would say that it does not: rejecting the belief, for instance, that swimming is the best of all possible physical exercises, does not entail that it is the worst. It is surprising that of all the critics who, in the space of nearly three-quarters of a century since the publication of the *Zibaldone*, have labelled Leopardi a pessimist, and have analyzed his pessimism into three phases of anthropologic, historical and cosmic pessimism, not one seems ever to have noticed the fairly obvious fact that the word *pessimismo* occurs only once in the *Zibaldone*, and that where it occurs, Leopardi used it to *deny* that he wished to replace optimism with pessimism. The previous paragraphs, beginning 'All is evil. Everything there is evil; for each thing to exist is evil; everything exists to an evil end...' etc. have been all too often quoted to demonstrate the depth of Leopardi's despair and the utterly negative quality of his philosophy. But the quotations stop short of the concluding paragraph:

> This system of thought, though it upsets our belief that the end [of existence] cannot be other than good, might perhaps be

easier to maintain than Leibniz's or Pope's belief that all is well. I would not, however, go as far as to say that the existing universe is the worst of all possible universes, replacing thus optimism with pessimism. Who can gauge the limits of possibility? (*Zib.* 4174)

About a year later, Leopardi again confirmed his qualified scepticism:
If we cannot judge the ends, nor possess sufficient data to know whether things in this universe are actually good or bad; whether what appears to be good is good, and what appears to be bad is bad; why should we say that the universe is good, on the basis of what seems to us good, and not that it is bad, on the basis of what seems to us bad, which is at least as much? Let us then refrain from judging, and let us say that this is a universe, that this is an order of things, but let us not say whether it is good or bad. Certainly for us, and as far as we are concerned, it is mostly bad ... (*Zib.* 4258)

Obviously Leopardi was personally convinced that the destiny of man is to suffer. The point is, however, that since man is only a tiny and insignificant part of the universe, he would be rash to erect his own particular view of the universe into a general and absolute statement about its goodness or badness. This is perfectly consistent with Leopardi's often repeated principle of relativism, that one cannot deduce true general consequences from true individual or circumscribed experiences (see the *Zibaldone* index s.v. *relatività*).

I think it is legitimate to call Leopardi a pessimist only if one gives this word a strongly positive meaning, as Luporini, Timpanaro and Binni have done in their studies. It is a fact, however, that the word has always been loaded with negative connotations, and with the derogatory meaning of someone 'unfamiliar with modern philosophy and not caring for progress, civilisation and enlightenment' (1, 184, 2). The label of pessimist has significantly contributed to the misunderstanding of Leopardi's virile determination 'to despise the cowardice of men and reject every consolation and every puerile deception, and have the courage to sustain the lack of all hopes, to look unflinchingly at the desert of life, not to ignore any part of human unhappiness and to accept all the consequences of a painful but true philosophy' (1, 181, 2). It has also distracted readers' attention from the object of his attacks, in Binni's words 'the century-old and present mystification of optimism, and of religious or promethean-humanistic pride' (1, lxxx), or, in other words, the attempt to secure the unlimited extension of individual well-being and privilege at the expense of the masses, as if it were possible to base individual happiness on mass exploitation, or mass happiness on individual unhappiness. Leopardi might have preferred to be called an anti-optimist, since he believed in the positive function of destructive philosophical systems (*Zib.* 2708–9). It is a falsehood to pretend that there is no value in a destructive, or revolutionary ideology because it does not present any positive solution. Let us hear Leopardi's view:

> In comparing ancient with modern philosophy the former is said to be superior, principally because ancient philosophers all wanted to teach and to be constructive, whereas modern philosophy generally does nothing but to demystify and to dismantle. …Modern philosophers always take away but put nothing in its place. And this is the true way of philosophizing; not, as some say, because the weakness of our intellect prevents us from discovering positive truths, but because, in fact, the knowledge of truth is nothing else but the removal of errors; and most wise is he who knows how to see the things he has before his own eyes, without attributing to them non-existent qualities. Nature lies unfolded before us, naked and open. To know her well it is not necessary to lift any covering veil: it is necessary to remove the obstructions and misconceptions which are in our eyes and in our minds, fabricated by ourselves and caused by our reason. (*Zib.* 2709–10)

9. 'The Soul of Everything is Contrast'

Mere possession of a scientific culture was not unusual for a poet. In the eighteenth century a large number of writers had their imagination fired by scientific discoveries, which they celebrated in didactic poems. Nearer Leopardi's time, Alfonso Varano, Giuseppe Parini, Vincenzo Monti and Cesare Arici (to mention only the better known poets whom Leopardi had studied and quoted) had all followed in the tradition of writing poems about science and progress (the invention of vaccination, the flight of the first hot-air balloons, the reclamation of marshland, electricity) or used scientific imagery in their verse. Conversely many scientists felt that their culture would not be complete unless they were able not only to write sonnets and odes, but also to expound their theories in verse. A notable example was the Jesuit Ruggero Giuseppe Boscovich (1711–87), astronomer, mathematician and physicist whose influence lasted well into the nineteenth and twentieth century (Leopardi quoted him in his *Storia dell'Astronomia*, I, 723; 726, 2). Boscovich was a member not only of famous scientific academies but also of the Arcadia, and spent twenty-five years of his life writing and revising a Latin poem, *De Solis ac Lunae defectibus*, which he then dedicated to the Royal Society. The name of Lorenzo Mascheroni (1750–1800) is remembered only for his verse description of the laboratories and botanical gardens of Pavia University (*Invito a Lesbia Cidonia*), whereas his scientific accomplishments have been forgotten.

But in either case the relationship between scientific contents and poetic forms was a purely external one, in that both those writers subscribed to the old conception of poetry as the art that achieves utility and moral edification through aesthetic delectation. Monti and his followers believed that the 'dry sciences could be made less dry by mythological ornamentation' (*Sermone sulla Mitologia*, Discourse on Mythology 1825) which reminds one of those nineteenth-century architects who felt that their railway stations would be aesthetically acceptable only if the dark satanic steam engines were hidden behind façades resembling Greek temples. Romantic poets and theorists had gone as far as to discard mythology but not much further. They did not really explain why literature had to concern itself with progress and science, if at all; nor did they satisfactorily formulate or solve the problem of what poetic form to use in order to express such contents, as Cesare De Lollis demonstrated in his *Saggi sulla forma poetica italiana nell'Ottocento*. Where Leopardi differed from them is that for him science was not a poetic content, nor was poetry a formal ornament. Science was the basis of his poetic methodology.

As I suggested at the beginning of this study (see p. 17 above), Leopardi was deeply concerned from the very beginning of his literary career with the relationship between form and content. Some of his thoughts on this problem appear in the *Zibaldone* as reflections on literary style. In *Zib.* 2049–51 he had stated that 'one can be a poet having no other poetic quality than style': but then his definition of style included images, and signified therefore a union of form and content (no defence of formalism can be inferred from those pages). About two years later he came back to the same point, and, this time distinguishing between style (considered merely as formal qualities) and ideas, images and emotions (seen as elements of content) he affirmed that 'no one can ever be a poet only because of his style, unless he is a poet also because of everything else' (*Zib.* 3389). Whatever the exact meaning and extension of 'style' at any given time, it seems clear that Leopardi did not wish to separate form from content in poetry, although, like everybody else, he found it expedient to distinguish between them.

However expedient that distinction may be, there is no contrast between form and content, since they are poles of a single mental continuum. We know for a fact that contents can only be realized as forms, deep structures (to use current linguistic terminology) can only appear as surface structures, and ideas and images can only be understood as words and sentences. Meanings must be expressed as organization of signs, and relationships of meaning as formal (logical or syntactic) connections. And yet we know as yet no way of representing that continuum as a process, of describing how contents appear as forms, how deep structures generate surface structures, how ideas and images turn into word and sentences. Semantics is still one of the least understood areas of linguistic scholarship. The content-form relationship is one of the various binary oppositions, polarities or dualities that since time immemorial have always fascinated and exercised the minds of philosophers. Leopardi was particularly attracted by the problems they raise. We have already briefly examined his solution of the spirit-matter dualism (p. 59 above). Among his notes for the *Operette* one finds the following quotation from Mme de Staël (*Corinne*, liv.14, ch. 1):

> Car il ne faut pas se le cacher, il y a deux côtés à toutes les manières de voir: on peut vanter l'enthousiasme, on peut le blâmer; le mouvement et le repos, la variété et la monotonie sont susceptibles d'être attaqués et défendus par divers arguments; on peut plaider pour la vie et il y a cependant assez de bien à dire de la mort ou de ce qui lui ressemble (1, 211, 2). [We should not hide from ourselves the fact that there are two sides to every opinion: one can praise enthusiasm, and one can condemn it; movement and rest, variety and monotony are susceptible of being attacked and defended by various arguments; one can make a plea for life, and yet there is something good to be said for death, or what resembles it.]

This quotation is not only the germ of the *Dialogo di un Fisico e di un metafisico*, but also a justification of the dialogic structure of most of the *Operette*. There is more, however, to Leopardi's fascination with contrast than the common notion that there are two sides to every question (often used to justify compromising between both, or to avoid choosing either).

Very early in his *Zibaldone* Leopardi began to probe the limitations of the Aristotelian principle of identity by exploring the acceptability of apparently contradictory propositions: the strong perception of the inevitability and necessity of boredom can kill boredom, fear and courage may coexist, muddle may be found together with clarity, the rarity of a thing may cause it to be wrongly valued; all of this discussed in the space of two pages (*Zib.* 262–3), which seems to indicate that he was not so much interested in the propositions themselves as in their logical properties. About a year later Leopardi was wrestling with one of the knottiest problems of theology, which can be summarized as follows. The orthodox Christian idea of a God who is both perfect and good is contradictory; if God were only good, and not also its opposite, his perfection would be incomplete, since there would be a mode of being which is denied to him. 'Absolute perfection embraces all possible qualities, also contrary ones, because contrast is not absolute, but relative' (*Zib.* 1626). This idea can be traced back to Spinoza (see p. 12 above). There must therefore be a distinction between the way in which God manifests himself to man (as wholly good), and the way in which he must necessarily exist (as synthesis of infinitely varied and contrasting ways of being) (*Zib.* 1637, 1643, 1646). Some of the attributes of God revealed by the Christian religion (e.g. his being one and three) contrast with the very principle of non-contradiction which seems manifestly inadequate to make sense of them. This proves not that revelation is false, but that our ways of thinking are only relatively true (*Zib.* 1627).

This manner of sidestepping the principle of non-contradiction soon led Leopardi to some rather extraordinary pronouncements about God: if he can exist in all possible ways he must also be above morality (*Zib.* 1637–42), and he may even be endowed with material existence (*Zib.* 2073–4). Leopardi made frequent disclaimers that his 'system' was in any way against religion; but that was only because his system, by admitting of irrational and contradictory ideas, by being a system that denied all systems, and even embraced atheism, was the only structure of thought that could accommodate the irrationality of religion (*Zib.* 1642–3). Soon Leopardi came close to discovering the dialectical method, which was being developed by his older contemporary Hegel. He realized that all contraries, truth and falsehood, substance and appearance, insensitivity and sensitivity, ice and fire, patience and impatience, impotence and power, mathematics and poetry, even his original pair of enemies, nature and reason, 'are essentially linked one to the other, and one cannot be considered separately from the other' (*Zib.* 1839, 1842). He did perceive the dynamic properties of contradiction (*Zib.* 2156); only he did not see them as part of an evolutionary historical process. He could not develop his discovery, like Hegel, in a way that would make the progress of the human spirit depend upon the conciliation of opposites and the composition of antinomies (and so-called social progress upon the smoothing over of social contradictions); and preferred to subsume it under his already asserted belief in epistemological relativism (*Zib.* 452). The final attacks against the principle of identity with copious references to the *Operette*, were entered in the *Zibaldone* in June 1824 and April 1825 (4099–4101 and 4127–32).

The question of antinomies and the difficulties caused by the identity principle are of primary importance in Leopardi's system. Of course, 'binary oppositions are intrinsic to the process of human thought. Any description of the world must discriminate categories in the form "p is what not-p is not"' (Leach). Man has a basic 'either-or', 'this-other' mode of perception, apparently biologically rooted in the individual's immediate awareness of himself as distinct from other objects and individuals. The fundamental experience of, and need for, his own identity, tells him that nothing can be at the same time itself and other than itself; beyond this certainty lies the anguish of madness. Man is also aware of a distinction between his own 'inner' self and its 'outside' appearance: an issue of particular importance for Leopardi who was physically misshapen (*Zib.* 207). Duality thus reproduces itself within identity. Any identifiable thing can therefore be perceived as a duality of components: inside and outside, soul and body, mind and matter, content and form, etc. And a duality of components, neither excluding the other, is often mistakenly perceived as a contrast of incompatible terms, 'this-other' being confused with 'either-or'. Some of Leopardi's binary oppositions, like reason and nature, or poetry and philosophy, went through an early stage when they were presented as irreconcilable, and only later were seen by him to be linked and complementary. This is the reason for many apparent contradictions in the *Zibaldone*.

The content-form duality (*signifié-signifiant*, to use Saussurian terms) and the identity principle are of crucial importance in language, the typically human symbolization-expression process, enabling man to make sense of the world, and to organize conceptually his own experience. In language the content-form relationship is not a fixed, bilateral one. A form may be charged with several contents (just think of the many meanings of the word 'nature'); conversely a content may find expression through several forms. Words are capable of indefiniteness, and phrases of ambiguity: we have seen the importance of these concepts for Leopardi's poetic theory (pp. 40–1). But no content can be exactly equivalent to any other content, nor can a form be represented by any other form: forms and contents are in themselves untranslatable. Meaning, being the continuum defined by content and form, necessarily transcends both. Knowing more than one language, and being a poet and translator, Leopardi was particularly aware of these issues, which form a considerable part of his speculation (see the index to the *Zibaldone* s.v. *lingua* etc., *traduzione, stile*).

Forms can be invariant, recursive, infinitely reproducible without substantial changes. On the other hand the fundamental identity of individual persons or objects appears to survive many observable changes of form. This accounts for one of the oppositions inherent in the concept of nature, which is in one sense the embodiment of the invariance, recursiveness and reproducibility of observable phenomena (the object of what was once called 'natural philosophy'), and in another sense the symbol of the time-bound evolution of living things, and change of inanimate things (the object of the comparatively recent discipline of 'natural history' popularized by the works of Buffon, which Leopardi knew well). The problem of how to relate fixed 'natural laws' or 'states' to historical change, lived through by man both phylogenetically and ontogenetically, was a very important one for scholars, like Leopardi, who had seen the whole emphasis of scientific thought in the eighteenth century shift gradually from the mathematico-mechanical conceptions of a changeless universe inherited from Descartes and Newton, to the new evolutionary theories of Buffon, Herder, and the various geologists of whom Leopardi had knowledge from Domenico Paoli's already quoted book.

One of the long-standing debates in Leopardian criticism concerns the alleged evolution in time and eventual contradictoriness of Leopardi's ideas of nature. As I have suggested (p. 18) it is in my view just as important to describe diachronic change as to study the underlying structural reasons that make such change possible. There is little doubt that in Leopardi's ideas one can perceive a change of emphasis, from a motherly and benign to an evil and hostile nature. But there is also no doubt that this shift of emphasis was possible because of the various dualities already inherent in the concept of nature, as it is conceptually structured and as it was historically formulated; and as Leopardi had inherited it from classical and eighteenth-century culture. After what we have observed so far about the importance of contrast as a dynamic element in Leopardi's philosophical system, it should be clear that to show him shifting, at any given time, between contrasting ideas and different viewpoints, is not intended to reduce his speculation to a mere expression of unreflected emotional states such as allegedly become a 'pure poet', but on the contrary to affirm the philosophical dignity of his thought, and his near-dialectic perception of the complex issues involved.

The changelessness of nature was affirmed by Leopardi in 1818 (*Discorso intorno alla poesia romantica*, 1, 918, 2; 930, 2) and in 1822 or even 1832 (*Frammento sul suicidio*, 1, 199, 2; where there seems however to be a distinction between a changeless *natura naturata* and a *natura naturans* producing changing and variable things, see also *Zib.* 118 and 129). In *Zib.* 1558–62, however, written in 1821, Leopardi elaborates on Monti's distinction between 'brute' and 'cultivated' nature, and admits that 'after changing himself, man had to change nature'. In those five pages one sees very clearly the co-existence of two notions of nature: a metaphysical extra-historical perfect nature compatible only with an ideal state of human perfection, but standing above and outside man, and a historical nature including man who has deviated from his ideal stage and has ended by changing nature itself. Both notions, of nature totally outside man, and of nature which 'not only surrounds us and crowds against us from every direction, but also lies within us, living and crying out', are present in the *Discorso* (p. 26). There cannot therefore be any question of a chronological development from one idea to the other.

These different viewpoints have necessarily different implications. On the one hand Leopardi must praise those ancient times when man was nearer his 'natural state'; and consequently present all subsequent departures from that state as a process of barbarity and corruption, coinciding with the development of the so-called civilization (*Zib.* 403–4, 4185). On the other hand, he understood history well enough to realise that the only life one can live is in the present, that nature can be rediscovered by civilized man only in civilization, and that to escape from the present is just another of those illusions that may help man to bear his sorrows only on condition that they are never confused with reality. As we have seen, both viewpoints are present in the *Discorso*; and eighteen years later Leopardi attempted to reconcile his declared preference for the ancients (*Zib.* 338) and his recognition of modern cultural and philosophical progress (*Zib.* 2705–9, 3318–22), not to speak of the several instances in which he recognized that the moderns were better than the ancients (*Zib.* 3469–71, 1976–8, 3482). No doubt, he also wished to reconcile the contrasting viewpoints about the consequences of a full and intense life for personal happiness expressed in the two dialogues *della Natura e di un Anima* and *di un Fisico e di un Metafisico*:

> The states in which the spirit (*animo*) is less developed, and therefore less lively, are the least sensitive, and therefore the least unhappy human states. This is why I prefer the primitive (*selvaggio*) to the civilized state. But, once the development of the spirit has begun and reached a certain stage, it is impossible to go backward, it is impossible, in the individuals as much as in the masses, to prevent progress. ... From the development and the liveliness of their spirits there follows a greater sensitivity, ... hence greater unhappiness. There remains only one remedy ... the greatest possible amount of activity, of action, occupying and filling the developed faculties and the life of the spirit ... This remedy is far from being equivalent to the primitive state, but

its effects are the best to be obtained, and the resulting state is the best possible one, once man has been civilized. (*Zib.* 4186–7)

One should remember in this connection Leopardi's psychological explanation why old people mistakenly indulge in praising the past (*Pensieri* XXXIX, I, 226–8), and conversely why one often imagines, equally wrongly, that life must have been uncomfortable and difficult in the past (*Zib.* 4198–9); summed up in one of Filippo Ottonieri's memorable sayings:

> Each generation believes, on the one hand, that the past was better than the present; on the other that peoples improve as they get further away, day by day, from their primitive state; if they went backward, no doubt they would get worse. (I, 145–6)

The point is, of course, that the word *progress* is ambiguous, since it implies not only the value-free notion of 'going forward' through historical time, but also two value-loaded extra-historical concepts, in which 'going forward' is seen either as an inherently good thing, or as a progressive 'moving away' from an initial state of perfection. Leopardi attempted to do away with this ambiguity and to dispose of the long-standing *querelle des Anciens et des Modernes* by suggesting that progress and civilization, in their value-loaded sense, are not functions of the passing of time: it would be wrong to consider our civilization better (or, one may add, worse) than the ancient *simply* because it came later (*Zib.* 4171–2).

There is a tie-up between these views of progress and the dual aspect of nature. In a pre-historic, or extra-historic state as posited by Leopardi, man as a species can only look upon nature as benign mother; but to the individual, ontogenetically conscious of a long developmental process that, by bringing about the refinement of reason and the progress of all his faculties, has removed him from his pristine, timeless, 'natural' state, nature can only appear as distant, and in the last resort unfriendly (*Zib.* 1530–1). The concept of nature is, in this respect, just as ambivalent as the concept of Mother. Once again there is no clear progression from one image to the other. The hostility between nature and the individual appears as early as 1820 in *La sera del dì di festa* (see p. 51 above). Conversely as late as February 1829 Leopardi denied that nature's designs were necessarily evil (*Zib.* 4461–2) (even if I agree with Timpanaro that those pages do not hark back to the early view of a beneficent nature). The point seems to me that, as Leopardi clearly said several times (e.g. *Dialogo della Natura e di un Islandese, Zib.* 4257–9),

nature itself is neither good nor bad, and our judgement of it is
bound to be partial. He had said the same things of God (see pp. 52,
76), and in *Zib.* 393 he had identified God and Nature: an equiva-
lence confirmed by his extension to nature of the Spinozian idea that
God must be endowed with all possible modes of existence. Nature
is therefore all there is, in all possible, actual and potential manners of
being, including contradictory ones (*Zib.* 4087, 4129, 4204–5). It is
the only possible absolute granted that, according to Leopardian
relativism, the only absolute foundation of all metaphysics is that all
is relative (*Zib.* 452, 1791–92), and nature is the concept including
all relativity. Its absoluteness is not *a priori*, but logically *a posteriori*.
Since all there is cannot be other than what it is, the concept of nature
acquires a tautological necessity, and perfection. But it is a necessity
that implies chance (*Zib.* 159–60, 583–4, 1570–2): nature could not
be different from what it is, even if it had chosen to be in any one of
an infinite number of random manners of existence. On the other
hand chance must imply necessity, since nature can only be the way
it is. The fact that it is possible to define the concept of nature logically on a metaphysical plane does not mean that nature is logically
determined on the physical plane. On the contrary, nature cannot
be reduced to mathematical formulae; the only sure thing about
nature's laws is that they are unknown (*Zib.* 4189); our reason tries
to exclude from the notion of overall general order the possibility of
particular accidents, but it does not follow that nature also excludes
it. Nature and reason are at variance because while nature necessarily
implies chance, and randomly implies necessity, reason can operate
only by eliminating chance from its logical mechanisms. But in this
respect the operation of reason, obliged to choose between various
and often opposite possibilities, is definitely unnatural; since it intro-
duces the concept of contradiction and oppositeness between categories, which, though necessary on the metaphysical plane is
misleading on the physical plane. This is a truth that science would
only discover long after Leopardi's death, when it was realized, for
instance, that however useful it may be to think of radiation in terms
either of particles or of waves, there was no way in which such a
distinction could be said to apply to physical reality.

One way of facing the problems and questions of life is to project
solutions and answers on to some allegedly transcendent metaphysical reality: creating aetiological myths like the Golden Age; or
setting up absolute concepts like God, Nature, Progress, which
appear definitory, explanatory and inherently true only because

they are tautological. According to the Bible, God defined himself 'I am that I am' (Exodus 3.14); Nature is everything there is because it is what it is; Progress is mankind progressing or 'going forward' through time, which is the inevitable fact of history.

These are mostly empty concepts, which is not a defect, but a most useful property of concepts allowing them to be used as repositories for a wide range of ideas that cannot be easily fitted into logically consistent conceptual frameworks. The postulate that meanings lie outside and above their signs makes the mythical-metaphysical approach unchallengeable. It is a static and inherently ritual world-view since it is founded on myths that are themselves projections of recurrent phenomena. Its explanatory power depends upon, and leads to, religious faith, worship of the past, acceptance of tradition, submission to authority.

Another way of facing the questions of life is to reject completely the use of metaphysics and of empty concepts, and to look for the explanation of reality in reality itself. This can often be a more powerful and 'scientific' approach. Its effectiveness, however, depends on what one means by 'reality'. If it is taken to mean 'what is capable of systematic observation and description' (excluding what can and must be provisionally packed into empty concepts because no intellectual frame-work exists as yet to fit it in), to know reality would come to mean 'to know what can be known', which is an equally tautological and certainly more sterile method, as it was proved by the shortcomings of naive rationalism and scientific positivism. Leopardi's own philosophical methodology developed, as we have seen, into a rigorously materialistic and scientific investigation of reality which *included* myths and metaphysical concepts, not as true descriptions of the objective state of things but as useful 'empty' conceptual tools (see p.60 above). It was a very powerful method, because, by extending the field of reality to mental constructs, myths and 'illusions' it was able to distinguish between the structure and properties of the mind and the structure and property of whatever was being investigated by the mind; powerful enough to understand, or at least to justify, the reasons for, and the cultural function of, the ritualistic-mythological views it superseded.

10. Memory and Memories

The dialectical contrast between philosophy and poetry seems also to be reflected in Leopardi's life. The end of his process of 'conversion' to philosophy in 1819 marked the beginning of a fruitful period of poetic activity lasting until 1823. The end of the second period of philosophical and scientific meditation leading to the publication of the *Operette* and the indexing of the *Zibaldone* in 1827 heralded Leopardi's return to poetry.

The dates also show a correlation between the beginning of Leopardi's poetic activity and certain reflective and introspective stages in his meditation, when his thought, long occupied by external problems began to turn inwardly on himself. The first *canzoni* were composed shortly after the beginning of Leopardi's self-analysis (see p. 14 above) while at the same time the poet was embarking on his first autobiographical project, *Ricordi d'infanzia e di adolescenza* [Memories of childhood and adolescence, 1819]. Of 65 explicitly autobiographical entries in the *Zibaldone* (as distinct from the large number of indirect references to personal experience indexed in the *polizzine a parte*; II, 1276) 45 occur before 1822, none between September 1823 and September 1826, and 14 after 1826. The reference to Giulio Rivalta being twenty-seven years old suggests that Leopardi's second autobiographical project, *Storia di un'anima* was begun at some time between July 1825 and 1826. The excessive depth and intensity of Leopardi's introspective phases may be judged from a passage of the *Zibaldone* written shortly before his second journey to Bologna in April 1827, in which he admitted his 'mistake in wishing to lead a life wholly and exclusively introverted, intending and hoping to find peace' to the point of spending days without uttering a sound (*Zib.* 4259–60). During the whole of his winter sojourn at home, as he confessed to Puccinotti (Letter of 21 April 1827; I, 1281, 1), he never once went out of doors. In such states of intense isolation, the exercise of memory was for Leopardi a practical means of keeping sane, in touch with reality, and overcoming the uneasiness he experienced in unfamiliar places, where his feeling of identity was threatened (*Zib.* 4286–7). The recollection of the past

was for him a source of pleasure (*Zib.* 1777, 4415), and an essential
ingredient of poetry (*Zib.* 4426). The best times he ever had in his
life were therefore the times of perfect happiness spent in literary
composition (*Zib.* 4417–18).

In November 1827 Leopardi left Florence for Pisa, which he found
very congenial, both because of the warmer climate and of the
pleasant surroundings. He liked the town so much that he could not
wait to let his family and friends know; and two days after his arrival,
on 12 November, he wrote four letters in praise of Pisa, to Paolina,
Vieusseux, Stella and Adelaide Maestri. Further praises of the tem-
perate climate and the amenities of the town were in his letter to
Monaldo of 24 December, and to Paolina of 21 January 1828. Two
days earlier Leopardi had noted in the *Zibaldone*:

> Memories of my life. The deprivation of all hope, immediately
> consequent on my coming in to this world, has little by little
> caused the extinction of nearly all my wishes. Now, circum-
> stances being different, hope is resurrected, and I find myself in
> the strange situation of having much more hope than desire,
> and more hopes than wishes etc. (*Zib.* 4301)

The next page written partly on 15 February, partly on 15 April
1828, contains further references to the interplay of memory, introspection and poetic composition:

> One of the most notable effects that I intend and hope will
> result from my verses is that they should kindle my old age with
> the warmth of my youth … that they should make me not only
> remember but also reflect upon the sort of man I was, and com-
> pare the present me to my old self; and finally that they should
> give me the pleasure one feels in enjoying and appreciating
> one's own work, and in admitting and rejoicing in the beauty
> and accomplishments of one's own son, with no other satis-
> faction than would arise from having fashioned one more thing
> of beauty; whether other people accept it as such or not. (*Zib.*
> 4302)

And on 2 May 1828 he wrote to Paolina:

> I have finished at last the Anthology of Italian poetry: and after
> two years I have written some verse this April; but really old-
> style verse, as my heart once used to make. (I, 1311–12)

The memory of childhood and the theme of stylistic neglect in
contemporary literature, which Leopardi had dealt with in *Il Parini,
ovvero della gloria,* and again in *Zib.* 4268–72 and 4301 (last paragraph, written on 5 February 1828) mingle in the first of Leopardi's

new poetic compositions, *Scherzo*, written on 15 February—it appears out of sequence in most editions of the *Canti*, beginning with the one published by Starita in Naples in 1835, as if Leopardi had thought it of too slight importance to come just before *Il risorgimento* [Resurgence], *A Silvia* and the other *grandi idilli* of 1829. And yet it is important for us to place it in its proper chronological order, as evidence of the connection in Leopardi's mind between autobiographical recollection ('When as a child I was apprenticed to the Muses...'), the craft of poetry ('one of them...showed me one by one all the tools of the craft and the various uses each of them was put to, in prose and in verse'), the habit of looking critically at the state of the art ('"Muse", I asked, "Where is the file?" The Goddess replied: "The file is worn out: now we do without"...') and his happier disposition, symbolized in the title.

The next poem, *Il risorgimento*, written between 7 and 13 April 1828 expressed the resurgence of hope in Leopardi's heart. It consists of twenty stanzas of two quatrains each. The last stress of each line falls invariably on the sixth syllable, but the first line of each quatrain has eight syllables (*settenario sdrucciolo*); the second and third are normal *settenari* and are joined by rhyme; and the last has six syllables (*settenario tronco*) and rhymes with the last line of the second quatrain. About that time (1, 378, 1) Leopardi had been reading Manzoni's *Inni sacri* and *Il cinque maggio* [The Fifth of May, on Napoleon's death]. That poem, and two of the 'Sacred Hymns', were written in a metre very similar to *Il risorgimento*, though with a different rhyme pattern. It is not surprising to find in *Il risorgimento* (ll. 41 and 37) two echoes from the first stanzas of *Il cinque maggio*:

Ei fu. Siccome immobile (cf. Leopardi: Qual fui! Quanto dissimile).

Così percossa, attonita (cf. Leopardi: Giacqui: insensato, attonito).

The same rhythmical scheme as in *Il risorgimento* had been used by eleven-year-old Leopardi in a *canzonetta*, written in the style of Metastasio, which shares with stanzas 12–14 of the later poem the theme of the peace of mind induced by the contemplation of nature: one of the 'long-lost emotions of his youth',

gli affetti ch'io perdei
nella novella età...

Leopardi's indebtedness to Metastasio, which has been obvious to most critics from De Sanctis to Bigi, is confirmed by the clear reference to his well-known poem 'Dovunque il guardo io giro/ Immenso Dio ti vedo' [wherever I gaze I see you, all-pervading

God] contained in the second half of stanza 12, which seemingly supports the identification between God and Nature that had taken place in Leopardi's mind.

Leopardi had a relatively high opinion of Metastasio, whom he considered possibly the only poet worthy of that name since Tasso (*Zib.* 702), and whose famous canzonetta *La libertà* [Freedom] he included in his *Crestomazia* (pp.229–31) under the title *Il cuor liberato dall'amore* [The heart freed from Love]. He had also included two poems by Parini, on a similar theme and in a similar metrical form (pp.269–70, 273–5). At the time Leopardi was writing *Il risorgimento* he had freed himself from a passion for Countess Teresa Carniani-Malvezzi, a 41-year-old poetess, whom he described in glowing terms in a letter to his brother Carlo of 30 May 1826:

> During the first days of our acquaintance I existed in a sort of delirium or fever. We have never spoken of love, except in jest, but live together in a tender and sensitive friendship, we are interested in each other, and enjoy an abandonment which is like love without anxiety…Nearly every night I spend with her the time from dusk to midnight, and it seems to me a moment.…This acquaintance marks and will mark a definite stage of my life, because it has disenchanted me with disen-chantment, has convinced me that there actually are in this world pleasures which I thought impossible, and that I am still capable of steady illusions, in spite of a deeply rooted know-ledge and habit to the contrary, and it has resurrected my heart, after a sleep, or rather a complete death lasting over many years. (I, 1254, 2)

The 'steady illusion' was to last only a few months. The countess soon grew bored with the intense young man, and apparently made fun of him to some of her friends. When he left for Recanati in October 1826 he wrote to her asking to be received: there is no record that he was. In April 1827, as he was about to return to Bologna, Leopardi received from her one of her translations, without a single word of accompaniment. On 21 May he wrote from Bologna to Antonio Papadopoli who had advised him to drop the Contessa:

> How can you even imagine that I should keep visiting that strumpet Malvezzi? May my nose drop off if I ever went back there or thought of going after I heard her gossip about me, and if I do not speak of her all the evil I can. Yesterday I came across her in the street and turned my face to the wall pretending not to see her. (I, 1283, 2)

And yet this intense and unfortunate love experience was not lost on the poet. It had resurrected his heart, and revived his ability to cherish illusions. What did it matter if no factual reality corresponded to them, no real love shone in Teresa's eyes?

E voi, pupille tremule
voi, raggio sovrumano
so che splendete invano,
che in voi non brilla amor.

Nessuno ignoto ed intimo
affetto in voi non brilla:
non chiude una favilla
quel bianco petto in sé.

Anzi d'altrui le tenere
cure suol porre in gioco;
e d'un celeste foco
disprezzo è la mercé.

Pur sento in me rivivere
gl'inganni aperti e noti;
e de suoi proprii moti
si maraviglia il sen.

Da te, mio cor, quest'ultimo
spirto, e l'ardor natio,
ogni conforto mio
solo da te mi vien.

[And you trembling eyes, superhuman rays, I know that you sparkle in vain, that no love shines in you. No hidden and intimate emotion shines in you. That white bosom contains no warmth. On the contrary, it will make fun of another's tender cares; scorn is the reward for a heavenly passion. And yet I feel that the well-known illusions have revived in me. My breast is amazed at its own thrills. This last dash of energy and my inborn ardour, all my comfort come only from you, my heart.]

The image of an insensitive and mocking Teresa, from which the poet is still able to distil the positive soothing illusions needed for his emotional resurgence, is paralleled earlier on in the poem by the ambivalent image of nature, discordant from his pleasant imaginations, deaf and devoid of compassion (st. 15), and yet the source of those very beginnings, emotions and 'sweet deceptions' which his 'inborn faculty' needs to soothe his anxiety (st. 14).

From another autobiographical reminiscence of 1 January 1821, we learn that the name of Teresa was so strongly associated with the memory of a hateful old woman Leopardi knew as a child that he was 'always unfavourably prejudiced' against any person of that name (*Zib.* 482–3). It must have been a very unpleasant memory, if Giacomo tried to eradicate it by trying to persuade himself that the name Teresa could belong 'to a young, beautiful and lovely woman'. There was indeed no trace of adverse prejudice in his overenthusiastic praise of Teresa Carniani-Malvezzi, even if the outcome of his relationship with her may have confirmed it. But in 1821 he had not yet met Countess Malvezzi, and the only Teresa he knew whom one may reasonably suppose to have been beautiful and lovely (for she was certainly young) was Teresa Fattorini, one of the daughters of the Leopardis' coachman, who died of consumption in 1818 (she was about one year older than Giacomo), three times remembered by the poet in his *Ricordi d'infanzia e di adolescenza*:

> Anacreontic odes composed by me by the balcony railings listening to the carts rolling towards the storehouse and to the merry dinner noises coming from the coachman's, while his daughter was ill; story of Teresa whom I knew little, and my interest in her, as in all those who die young, since I was waiting for death myself; my dislike of poetry and the way in which I recovered from it...

> ...my fear of oblivion and total death, see *Ortis* 25 May 1798, near the end; morning song by a woman as I awoke, the coachman's daughters' song, particularly Teresa's while I was reading il Cimitero della Maddalena (1, 361, 2; 362, 1; also 363, 2).

The reference is to the Italian translation, published with the false imprint of Peking 1804, of *Le cimetière de la Madeleine* (1800) by Jean-Baptiste Joseph Innocent Regnault-Warin, better known as the author of one of the stories about The Man with the Iron Mask (*L'homme au Masque de fer*, 1804), and whose books Leopardi had been reading as early as 1812 (1, 574, 1). *The graveyard of the Madeleine* is a romantico-political hotchpotch about the French royal family, seen as the sacrificial victim of the 1789 revolution; the sort of pro-royalist novel popular during the Restoration, which one would expect to find in Monaldo's library. Giacomo used it as a source book for the tragedy *Maria Antonietta* which he began to write on 30 July 1816, and found it very moving. He also used it as emotional stimulus for his meditations on death, of which he speaks at length in his *Ricordi*. In this respect, however, the most important reference was to Foscolo's *Ortis*, which, as we know, is the story of a young man's impossible love for a girl called Teresa. Jacopo's letter of 25 May 1798 is a very important one, since it contains many themes later worked into *I sepolcri*, including the consoling idea that death does not mean total oblivion; and it brings to a conclusion the sad story of Lauretta, particularly meaningful to Leopardi, who was obsessed with the idea of the death of young people. The letter ends with Jacopo's vision of his own tomb, visited by Teresa at dawn for a last farewell.

Thus a French tear-jerking novel, the story of a young man's love for a girl called Teresa, Teresa Fattorini's morning song and the all-pervading theme of untimely death formed a sort of emotional knot in Leopardi's mind that would be untangled only in his mature years; at a time when, as nearly twelve years before, he was recovering, if not from a dislike of poetry, at least from a barren period during which he had written none. The best antidote to the image of the strumpet Malvezzi, already exorcised in *Il risorgimento*, was the image of that other Teresa, evidence that the name could indeed belong to a lovely girl. An image probably evoked by the fact that the sister-in-law of Giuseppe Soderini, Leopardi's landlord in Pisa, was a lovely young girl called Teresa Lucignani with whom Leopardi was on familiar terms ('God forbid I should call him Signor Conte' Teresa told a journalist in her old age, 'he wanted to be called Giacomo'). But the name of the beautiful image was changed. It is not Teresa, but Silvia:

> Silvia, rimembri ancora
> quel tempo della tua vita mortale
> quando beltà splendea
> negli occhi tuoi ridenti e fuggitivi,
> e tu lieta e pensosa, il limitare
> di gioventú salivi?
> [Sylvia, do you still remember that time of your mortal life, when beauty was shining in your smiling and elusive eyes, and you, full of joy and wonder, approached the threshold of your youth?]

The poem opens with the theme of memory, signified semanti-cally by the word *rimembri* and structurally by the line *negli occhi tuoi ridenti e fuggitivi*, reminding the reader of *fuggitivo riso* found in an 1816 poem entitled *Le rimembranze* [Memories] and of *l'occhio…fuggitivo e vago* in ll. 85–86 of the 1817 poem *Il primo amore*, in memory of Giacomo's first love for his father's cousin Gertrude

Cassi-Lazzeri. The connection between first love and shy fleeting
glances had already appeared in st. 8 of *Il risorgimento*:

> E voi pupille tenere
> sguardi furtivi, erranti
> voi de'gentili amanti
> primo, immortale amor…

(There are further connections between lines 15 and 19 of *A Silvia*
and lines 76 and 42 of *Il primo amore*, first published in 1826.)

All this thinking backwards to the springtime of life, the happy
and hopeful time of one's adolescence could not take place in
Leopardi's mind, so keen on contrast, without his considering as
often before (e.g. *Zib.* 4241–3) the illusory nature of the praises of
one's youth. Castiglione had pointed this out in a passage from book
II of *The Courtier*, which Leopardi had included in the 'speculative
philosophy' section of his 1827 prose anthology; and this passage,
as Giulio Bollati has shown, in a convincing and illuminating
demonstration of the close connection between philosophy and
poetry in Leopardi's work, is the source of many key words and
expressions in *A Silvia*. Silvia is the *figura*, that is the real-life metaphorical analogue of Leopardi's *lacrimata speme* (l.55), which, seen
from the viewpoint of one's adolescence looking forward to the
future, is hope (ll. 22, 29, 50), but contemplated as a memory during
one's mature years, is an illusion (ll. 32–5) destined to fade away
before the bitter truth (ll. 60–1). Leopardi, who began his poem by
addressing his memory of a dead girl, ends it by questioning the
'dear companion of my youth' who is not Silvia but his by now
defunct youthful hope of which Silvia's tomb is the symbol. 'Even
Hope, the last Goddess, deserts tombs' Foscolo had written in *I
sepolcri*. Hopelessness was the necessary counterpart, in Leopardi's
model of nature as a synthesis of contrasts, of the resurgence of
hopes which his new poetry was celebrating.

There are considerable affinities between *A Silvia* and *Le ricordanze*
[Memories], composed between 26 August and 12 September 1829.
Bollati has shown that this poem too bears clear echoes of Castiglione's passage. Nerina could be an etymological variation of Silvia
(*Nerina*<NEMORINA<NEMUS, meaning 'wood' like SILVA) and
it is well known as the name of Silvia's friend in Tasso's *Aminta*. The
poem amplifies and develops the motifs of *A Silvia*. The picture of
life at the father's house is more detailed (ll. 3–5; 17–19; 61–76).
Greater tenderness is shown to the transfigured image of Teresa (ll.
136–73). The theme of lost hopes is expanded (ll. 77–103). The

search into the poet's memory goes deeper and resurrects images from *La vita solitaria* (ll. 63–4) which it resembles in its superficially disconnected structure; from *L'infinito* (ll. 19–24); from the early *Zibaldone* (l. 50; *Zib.* 36, reminding one of *Zib.* 1531–2, 1 and the 'hidden link' discussed in ch. 3); from an 1811 poem with the significantly contrasting title *La dimenticanza* [Forgetfulness], the beginning of which anticipates lines 10–15 of *Le ricordanze* and ties up the poem more firmly with *Zib.* 1 and the passage from *Ricordi* about Teresa and the squashed firefly (1, 363, 2):

> Nel tempo in che dileguasi
> All'orizzonte il rosso,
> Quando più forte gracida
> La rana dentro il fosso:
> Allor che gli astri brillano
> Nel cielo azzurro e puro,
> E splendono le lucciole
> Sul verde suolo oscuro
> Allor che ad ogni piccolo
> Romor che fa il viandante
> Gl'inquieti cani abbaiano
> Ai casolari innante. ...

[At the time when the red hues fade away on the horizon, when the frog croaks louder in the ditch, when the stars sparkle in the clear blue sky and the fireflies glitter in the darkness on the green soil, when at any small noise made by the traveller the listless dogs bark before the farmhouses. ...]

The belief that memory is the source of poetic images appears frequently in the pages of the *Zibaldone* written during Leopardi's last stay in Recanati (4426–7, 4449–50, 4471, 4485, 4492, 4495, 4513, 4515), and inspires all the poems written during that period. In *La quiete dopo la tempesta* [The quiet after the storm], written towards the end of September 1829, Leopardi recalls with great effectiveness and economy of detail, the end of a storm over Recanati, as an illustration of his principle that pleasure arises mostly out of the cessation of anxiety. Similarly in *Il sabato del villaggio* [Village Saturday] written on 29 September, he describes the feeling of joyous anticipation of the holiday among the townsfolk, as an illustration of the idea often repeated in the *Zibaldone*, and succinctly expressed by a quotation from Rousseau, that 'one is only happy before being happy' (*Zib.* 4492). In both poems one can see beautiful glimpses of Recanati landscape and life, oddly contrasting with the 'inhuman dwelling place' described in ll. 28–49 of *Le ricordanze*. But it is precisely because the present Recanati appeared so horrible to him that Leopardi had to replace it with a mental image of Recanati from the past, according to the principle that beauty lies only in objects remembered, or seen in one's imagination:

> To a sensitive and imaginative man who lives, as I lived for a long time, continuously feeling and imagining, the world and its objects are, so to speak, double. He will see with his eyes a tower, the countryside; he will perceive with his ears the sound of a bell; and at the same time he will see in his imagination another tower, another countryside, and will hear a different bell. All the beauty and pleasure of things lies in this second series of objects. (*Zib.* 4418)

Torre, *campagna*, the sound of bells, together with the main themes of the next six pages of the *Zibaldone*, written in December 1828 (the poet's loneliness, his solitary walks, the inability of man to achieve in his youth the social success he will no longer enjoy later in life) are the principal motifs of *Il passero solitario* [Lonely sparrow] for which there is no precise date of composition. The poem appeared in print for the first time in the 1835 edition, where it preceded *L'infinito*. The title dates from a group of notes to be used in future poems, written in 1819, and for this reason it was long included in the 1819–21 group of *idilli*. It is now clear, because of stylistic and other reasons, that it does not belong to that group and that it is closely related to the *canti* of 1829–30. Its metrical structure is unlike anything written before *A Silvia*. Line 37 is similar to line 13 of *Le ricordanze*. The description of the holiday in lines 27–35 evokes the atmosphere of *Il sabato del villaggio*: only in these two poems do we find the impersonal *odi* (*Passero* ll. 8, 29, 30, *Sabato* ll. 25, 33). Finally, if one reads the 1819 *Argomenti d'idilli*:

> Galline che tornano spontaneamente la sera alla loro stanza al coperto. Passero solitario. Campagna in gran declivio veduta alquanti passi di lontano e villani che scendendo per essi si perdono tosto di vista. ... Donzellette sen gian per la campagna. ... (followed by notes for the description of a storm). [Hens coming back by themselves at dusk to their covered hen-house. Wide spread of sloping fields seen from some distance and peasants who, walking downwards, are lost to sight... The young girls were walking about the countryside. ...]

it is clear that the lonely sparrow is in the company of the hen (*gallina tornata in sulla via*) from *La quiete dopo la tempesta* and the young girl from *Il sabato*; and that those notes are the germ of all three poems. The contents of *Il passero* leads one to suppose that it was written in Recanati during the Spring (ll. 5–6) at the time of a religious festival which cannot therefore be the feast of San Vito (19 June) mentioned by most commentators, and must be the feast of the Santissima Annunziata (25 March) named several times by Leopardi in the dates of his *Zibaldone*, or San Giuseppe (19 March) or a movable feast of the Easter cycle. If one accepts that the contents of the poem reflect the time of its composition, then it must have been written either between *A Silvia* and *Le ricordanze* (Spring 1829) or after *Il sabato del villaggio* (Spring 1830). This however raises the question why was it not included by Leopardi in the 1831 edition, from which Leopardi explicitly excluded, of his written poems, only those he intended to reject (Letter to L. de Sinner of May 1831; I, 1358, 2). On that basis some critics have suggested a later date (from 1831 up to 1835), which one would have to reconcile with the poem's intimate connection with those of the 1828–30 group. It seems to me that, although the later date is perfectly possible, their reasons for suggesting it are not very convincing. The fact that the poem was included in the 1835 edition proves that it was written before that date, but the fact that it was not included in the 1831 edition cannot be evidence that it was not written before 1831. Furthermore, whatever answer one could give to the question why it was not included would make sense only assuming that it had been written; but the fact that no answer could be given would not prove that it was not. In any case there is no reason to disregard the positive evidence linking the poem to those of 1828–30. My choice of date for *Il passero solitario* is Spring 1830, without, of course, discounting earlier drafts or later revisions. Some critics have argued that the *passero solitario* is not a lonely sparrow at all, but a particular member of the thrush family, the blue rockthrush (*Monticola solitaria*), known for nesting in isolation in high places. It is of course possible that the bird seen by the poet on the top of the bell tower of the church of Sant'Agostino was indeed a blue rockthrush and not a common sparrow (*Passer Italiae*). The point of the poem, however, is the similarity between the isolation of the bird on a high place from which it can survey the scene around, and the loneliness of the poet which heightens his spiritual and emotional sensitivity; a point already made by Petrarch in his sonnet CCXXVI *Passer mai solitario in alcun tetto* quoting Psalm 102, which the Revised Version translates: 'I am like a pelican of the wilderness: I am like an owl of the desert. I watch and am as a sparrow alone upon the house top'. This point would be completely lost if *solitario* were considered as part of the scientific name of the bird (which Leopardi, who theorized the poetic value of indefinite words as opposed to precise terms, would not use in a poem), and not as an adjective indicating aloneness or loneliness.

Il sabato del villaggio gives another example of Leopardi's lack of precision. It irritated Pascoli (who was perhaps a good poet but definitely a bad critic) because roses and violets, which blossom at different times, are mixed in the same posy. Quite apart from Leopardi's *poetica dell'indefinito*, Pascoli overlooked the fact that *rose e viole* have blossomed together in countless Italian poems from Petrarch onwards (see examples in Leopardi's *Crestomazia: poesia* from Poliziano, p.14; Rucellai, p.22; Alamanni, p.54; Bernardo Tasso, p.56; Testi, p.152). Pascoli's lexical expertise should have told him that *rose e viole* appeared so frequently together because they were among the very few names of common flowers available in literary Italian, since most of the others existed only in the Italian dialects, and had only a limited regional currency.

It would be possible to muster an impressive number of references to solitary sparrows (Pulci, Pamfilo Sasso, Cellini, and others) storms (Alamanni, Menzini) and village *donzellette* and spinning *vecchierelle* (Brunelleschi, Fortiguerri from *Crestomazia: poesia*; Redi, Chiabrera and of course Petrarch) to show Leopardi's indebtedness to poetic tradition. It is perhaps more important to notice the way Leopardi managed to transform even quotations from other poets into something unique to his own poetry, profoundly original, devoid of any imitativeness: and to notice means not merely to observe that he did so, but to try to understand *how* he did it. Once words and expressions from poetic tradition have become a part of that close and intricate network of connections and cross-references between the *Canti*, they must necessarily acquire a typical Leopardian flavour. In reading about the hopeful *garzoncello* and the *donzelletta* one does not so much think of the countless times one comes across these words in Italian literature, as that they can be found within a few lines of each other in *La vita solitaria* (48, 59) as well as in *Il sabato*. In reading about Silvia-Teresa singing and weaving (*A Silvia* 20–2) one is not only reminded of Circes's night work in Aeneid VII, 11–14,

> … Solis filia lucos
> adsiduo resonat cantu …

arguto tenuis percurrens pectine telas
[The daughter of the sun makes the woods ring with her cease-
less song, while with the strident sley she sweeps along the fine-
spun warp.]

(lines which Leopardi had quoted in his *Discorso intorno alla poesia
romantica*, I, 934, 1), but also of a similar picture of a girl (the same
girl?) in *La vita solitaria* 63–6, where the Virgilian adjective *arguto* is
transferred from the weaver's sley to the girl's song.

Here is another example of how Leopardi used and transformed
poetic tradition. The word *errore*, as documented in the *Grande
Dizionario della lingua italiana* (vol. V, 1972, 265–8) belongs to two
main semantic fields, 'wavering motion' and 'misapprehension'.
Only in the former case, speaking for instance of fluttering petals or
gentle breezes, could it be accompanied by adjectives having a positive meaning (one finds *vago errore* in Petrarch and Menzini, and
dilettosi errori in Bernardo Tasso). Leopardi, on the other hand
applied adjectives like *felice, ameno, dilettoso, beato, leggiadro, gentile* to
errore taken with the latter meaning. Thus *dilettosi errori*, though a
quotation from the past, acquired a totally new sense. The same, or
similar adjectives (*lieto, dolce, ameno, gentile, caro, dilettoso*) are found
in the *Canti* in conjunction with the word *inganno*. Combinations of
both *errore* and *inganno* with a 'positive' adjective occur 14 times in
the *Canti*; and they are Leopardi's own way of expressing the concept of *illusione*, a word he never used in any of his poetic works
probably because he considered it a technical, philosophical term. In
a corpus of 41 canti a combination of this kind occurring 14 times
there are 15 more separate occurrences of *errore* and 4 of *inganno*)
must be considered as having a fairly high frequency, which indirectly confirms its stylistic significance.

A list of the 50 most frequent words or semantic fields (SF) found
in the *Canti* amounts to a sort of conceptual and stylistic profile of
Leopardi's lyrical poetry. The highest number of occurrences (614) is
totalled by first person (including plural with singular reference)
personal pronouns. Next come the SF's *morire* (*mortale, morte, morto*)
with 144 and *vivere* with 120. *Altro* and *ma* follow with 94 each: evidence of Leopardi's interest in contrast and opposition. Then *core*
(85); *amore* (70); *vedere* (68); *cielo* (66) and *terra* (64), very evenly
balanced; *giorno* (60), *età* and *tempo* (59 each), to which one should
add *dì* (40) and *anno* (35); the SF *fato* (64); *dire* (59); *natura* and the
SF *speranza* (56); *umano* (52); the SF *solitudine* (50); *petto* (49);
mondo (47); the SF *nascere* and *pensiero* (46); *dolce* (43); *caro* (42);

novello, novo (37); *affanno, cosa* and *occhio* (36 each); the SF *felicità* (34); *mirare, misero* and *uomo* (33 each); *antico* (32); the SF *piangere* and the SF *opra, lavoro* (31); *dolore,* the SF *giovinezza, mai, notte* and *vero* (30 each); *bello* and *sentire* (29 each); *campo* (28); *alto* (27), the SF *aria,* the SF *eterno* (26); and *luna* (25). Lower down the list, but with frequency above 10, one finds *vano, affetto, vento, cura, male, beltà, canto, diletto, seno, deserto, infinito, sogno, sereno, vago, estremo, immenso, celeste, donna, duro, infelice, campagna, conforto, invano, Italia, acerbo.* The total size of Leopardi's vocabulary used in the *Canti* is relatively small. Whereas an average school dictionary contains between 30,000 and 40,000 words, and an educated, articulate person, is said to use about 5,000, a rough count of the entries in the concordances for the *Canti* gives about 3,500 lexical items. The two existing concordances provide ample material for sophisticated investigations taking into account not only single fields and items but also their co-occurrence, which could yield very interesting results. I think they would confirm the general opinion that Leopardi achieved his complex poetic effects and his stylistic originality with the utmost economy of lexical and rhetorical means. In that respect he was rather similar to Petrarch, a poet he did not particularly like (he agreed with Lord Chesterfield's opinion that Petrarch was 'a sing-song love-sick poet', *Zib.* 4249), but whom he constantly studied from a stylistic and technical point of view; particularly between September 1825 and June 1826 when he prepared a commentary on the *Rime* for A. F. Stella.

At the same time as he was compiling commentaries and anthologies of the classics, Leopardi was interested, as he had been since his early youth, in the problems that occupied the minds of all Romantics. While he was in Florence in 1828 he focused his attention on the long-debated question of popular poetry, and of the Homeric poems. He consulted scholars, including the English George Frederick Nott (*Zib.*4322; 1, 1344, 2) known for his edition of Wyatt and Surrey and his Italian version of the Book of Common Prayer. He availed himself of the books and magazines of the Vieusseux Reading Room. A large section of the *Zibaldone* for this year is devoted to such problems as the distinction between naturalness, typical of art's infancy (and of children's art) and simplicity which is the result of refined craftsmanship (*Zib.* 4326–7); or the real nature of epic poems, which began in Homer's times as short *canti,* or hymns, and reached their later conglomerate form mainly through chance (*Zib.* 4327, 4356). Particularly stimulating are his remarks on the conditions of poetry before the invention of writing and the diffusion of literacy. Memory was then not only the source of poetic images but also the means for the transmission of the poetic text. How much more effective the ancient mode of publication of poetry was, when poets recited it before the people, than the modern one, when the printed text is circulated amongst a few hundred *cognoscenti* and never reaches the people (*Zib.* 4345–7).

Such meditations on popular poetry in the mainstream of Romantic thought gave Leopardi his inspiration for the *Canto notturno di un pastore errante nell'Asia*, composed between October 1829 and May 1830. The unusual title (Night Song of a Wandering Asian Shepherd) was derived from one of Leopardi's sources of information on popular poetry, the *Voyage d'Orenbourg a Boukhara* by Baron von Meyendorff. Giacomo spent a long time composing it because he wanted it simple and yet rich in meaning, like those ancient hymns which he had himself imitated in his youth (see p. 9). He wanted it to be popular: therefore the poem had to deal with fundamental issues about life and nature, of immediate relevance and universal importance. No wonder the *Canto notturno* harks back from the outset to the most intense period of philosophical meditation in Leopardi's life: the insistent questions appearing at intervals about the purpose and end of man's life in the universe are the same as Leopardi had asked himself in the *Operette morali* and summed up in the *Epistola* to Pepoli (there are other echoes of the *Epistola* in the poem). The initial simile between human life and the old man's catastrophic journey is the versification, in spite of its surface Petrarchan references, of a note in the *Zibaldone* (4162–3) written shortly before that same *Epistola*. Though occasioned by the discussion of Romantic issues, the poem is classical in style. Those typical word-images, *luna, vaga, mirare, solinga, affanno, noia,* connect the *Canto notturno* to the semantic and emotional network embracing the whole of the *Canti*. The poem can thus be seen as the culmination of a creative period, the summing up of Leopardi's poetic and philosophical beliefs after one of the richest and most interesting periods in his uneventful life, a worthy testament before he left his home, never to return.

11. Love and Death

The final blow to Leopardi's hopes of financial independence came, as we saw earlier (p. 66) in February 1830, when the *Accademia della Crusca* awarded its prize to Carlo Botta. And yet he was determined to leave Recanati, as he wrote to Vieusseux on 21 March: would it be possible for him to find some sort of work in Florence? In the meantime Leopardi's Florentine friends had decided to do something in his favour. His letter to Vieusseux crossed with one from the Neapolitan political refugee Pietro Colletta, inviting Leopardi to come and settle in Florence and informing him that a fund, anonymously subscribed, would guarantee him a monthly allowance of 18 *francesconi* (enough for him to live on) for a year from April 1830. Leopardi immediately accepted the invitation and left Recanati on 29 April. He spent a few days in Bologna on the way and reached Florence on 10 May. There, in spite of his ailing health, he began to prepare an edition of the *Canti*, which was advertised in July. He was introduced by Alessandro Poerio, another Neapolitan refugee, to Fanny Targioni-Tozzetti, the twenty-six-year old wife of a well-known scientist, well-known herself for her beauty, charm and the reputed number of her lovers. One of those who eventually won her favours was Antonio Ranieri, another Neapolitan gentleman who found the political atmosphere of Florence more tolerable than that of his home town. Leopardi had met him in 1827 and become his friend.

Both Fanny and Ranieri played a very important rôle in Leopardi's final years. Their relationship *à trois* was rather complicated. Leopardi, who desperately needed an emotional attachment after leaving his family, fell in love with Fanny. How far did she go in returning his affection? It is difficult to say. Certainly she found Ranieri more attractive. For all his artistic and intellectual gifts, Leopardi was not the sort of person who could appeal to women. And that was due not only to his physical deformity. He was subject to bouts of a form of psoriasis, when his skin would flake off and the cracks ooze serum. Because of this, and of his sensitivity to cold, he washed infrequently and changed his underclothes and shirt none too often. His various intestinal complaints gave him bad breath. As

Fanny herself put it in her old age, 'he stank'. One knows about these unpleasant traits of Leopardi's personality also from Antonio Ranieri, who late in life published a book of memoirs on his seven-year long cohabitation with the poet (*Sette anni di sodalizio con Giacomo Leopardi*; Milan 1880). The book gives a one-sided, ungenerous, and overall inaccurate account of their relationship, but there is no reason to doubt the truth of these details. While Leopardi was attracted to Fanny, Fanny was attracted to Ranieri, and Ranieri was head over heels in love with an actress from Bologna, Maddalena (Lenina) Pelzet whom he followed on her travels. Some of Fanny's affection for Antonio, unable to reach its absent object, must have rebounded on his friend Giacomo. Likewise, all Giacomo's love, which Fanny could not or would not accept, was to be transferred onto Fanny's lover, Antonio. This fairly common 'rebound' phenomenon explains why most of the letters Leopardi wrote to Ranieri during his absence from Florence in 1832–3, even taking into account Romantic sentimentality, read like the letters one might write to a lover: '...My soul...I clasp you to my heart no end....I send you a million kisses' (1, 1393, 1); '...I love you as only you can know, and would give my eyes to console you, if that could help. I embrace you as my only *causa vivendi*' (reason for living: 1, 1393, 2); '...as we must be joined together forever, since I want to follow you in any part of this world or of the next, do not jeopardize such bliss through haste...Farewell, my only inestimable treasure...' (1, 1395, 2). And more on this tone. There was enough for some biographers to suggest a homosexual attachment between Giacomo and Antonio—a rather misleading and unnecessary hypothesis, unless one wishes to stick that label on any cohabiting pair of the same sex. Fanny, who remained their friend until the end, called them *eterni legittimi compagni* [forever lawful companions] and was afraid Giacomo's melancholy and pessimism might dampen Antonio's zest for life. In fact Antonio probably found his zest for life stimulated and justified by the contemplation of Giacomo's melancholy life style. And Giacomo, who was denied any outlet for his emotions, lived them vicariously through Antonio's romantic and sexual exploits.

What we know of Leopardi's love for Fanny was consummated in poetry. There was no delicate irony this time about the illusion of love for a 'woman who cannot be found'. It was no passing infatuation for a teaser and a gossip like 'that strumpet Malvezzi'. It was an obsessive passion for a woman who combined the irrestible appeal

of her known availability to other men with a feeling of sincere and
lasting affection for him, and other not negligible virtues such as
simplicity of character, intelligence without affectation, a seemingly
fulfilled family life. This passion became Leopardi's uppermost
thought, *Il pensiero dominante*, as he described it in the first of four
poems written between 1831 and 1834:

> Dolcissimo, possente
> dominator di mia profonda mente;
> terribile ma caro
> dono del ciel; consorte
> ai lúgubri miei giorni
> pensier che innanzi a me sì spesso torni.
> [Most sweet thought, powerful lord of my innermost mind,
> awe-inspiring but dear gift of heaven; companion of my mourn-
> ful days, who so often come back before me...]

This time Leopardi was not addressing a disembodied image of
beauty, as in *Alla sua donna*, but the very reality of his love embodied
in his thought, in tones that remind one very forcibly of Dante's
image of Love in the second and third chapters of *Vita Nuova* as a
powerful Lord and Master: '*Ecce deus fortior me qui veniens domina-
bitur mihi*...una figura d'uno segnore di pauroso aspetto' (Here is a
god stronger than me who will come and rule over me...the image
of a Lord with a fearful countenance). In Dante's vision Love brings
about forebodings of death: he feeds the lover's heart to his beloved before taking her away from him. In Leopardi's poem, death
is also repeatedly mentioned to make the point that love is the only
thing that makes life preferable to death (ll. 85–7) and that it will
last until death comes (116–20). To say that the juxtaposition of
Eros and Thanatos is a traditional motif in poetry and figurative art,
(frequent, for instance, in emblem books) is not enough to justify
its use by Leopardi, unless we can show why it is a traditional motif
and Leopardi accepted it from tradition at this point. The juxtaposition of Death and Love makes sense only if Love is seen, not
merely as sentimental pining at a distance but as a life-giving force,
that is as sensual and sexual love, fulfilled and fulfilling. Since it
generates life, this physical love abolishes the fear of Death (ll. 44–6),
because at the same time it presupposes Death as the *necessitade estrema*,
the ultimate consequence (l. 50); for it follows naturally that any
living creature generated through physical love must eventually die,
and that when the life-giving force of love ebbs away one is then
ready for death.

Whenever love entails the fear of death, it is because those experiencing it are basically afraid to love fully and physically: that is typical of certain religious aberrations according to which love-making is seen as a degrading act occurring, as Saint Augustine put it, 'inbetween piss and shit'; and therefore sexual love is considered, like death, as leading towards corruption. But the connection between Eros and Thanatos can also be seen in a different, positive light, as the affirmation of the perennial regeneration of life. 'It takes great strength' wrote Georges Bataille in his extremely perceptive essay *L'affinité de la reproduction et de la mort*, 'to perceive the link between the promise of life, which is the meaning of eroticism, and the luxuriant aspect of death. Mankind is united in rejecting the concept that death is also the youth of the world. With a blindfold over our eyes we refuse to see that only death ensures an incessant burgeoning without which life would decline....Sexuality and death are the high points of a feast which nature celebrates with the inexhaustible multitude of beings, both signifying the unlimited waste by which nature runs counter to the wish to endure which is proper to each being'. There are many other passages (which would take too much space to quote in full) strongly reminiscent of Leopardi's concept of the cycle of life and death expressed in *Zib.* 1531, and of the unlimited waste of nature described in *Zib.* 4175–7. Such ideas must have come back to his mind when writing some notes for a hymn to Ahriman, the God of Evil in the Zoroastrian religion, probably in Spring 1833. The notes begin with four lines structurally similar to the first lines of *Il pensiero dominante* because of a series of *enjambements* placing the important concepts at the beginning of each line, and continue in prose: 'production and destruction etc.; in order to kill it gives life etc.; system of the world, all suffer [ing]' (1, 350, 2).

The conjunction of love and death, which appeared only indirectly in *Il pensiero dominante*, was openly theorized in the next poem, *Amore e morte*. Love and Death are siblings. They are the most beautiful things in the world. One gives the greatest well-being and pleasure, the other takes away all suffering. Death is no longer imagined by the poet as the usual skeleton portrayed in Mediaeval *Totentanzen*, and in the paintings by Nicolas Deutsch and Hans Baldung, while it is kissing a beautiful girl: death becomes 'a most beautiful girl herself, sweet to look at, not such as fearful people portray her' (ll. 10–12). If there is anything that inspires fear it is this dreary world, which our eyes, opened up by the impact of emotions, show us as an uninhabitable unhappy desert (ll. 27–

39). Once again the powerful life-death image of the sea returns, in a context containing clear references to *L'infinito* (the expression *il suo pensier figura* reminiscent of *io nel pensier mi fingo*, the words *spaura* and *quiete* in identical rhythmical placements). Only this time it is not an image of peaceful nirvanic ecstasy, but a symbol of stormy emotions and blinding passion (ll. 40–4). We must remember that Leopardi's classically composed style could not allow realistic surface descriptions but worked only through the skilful arrangement of traditional images. Lines 27–55 may seem to be a conventional picture of a lover tormented by platonic love pains; but, quite apart from the fact that Leopardi rejected that kind of platonism, the images are fairly typical of physical, sensual passion (*Il fier disio, la formidabil possa, l'invitta cura, l'affannoso amante, abbandonando all'alba il corpo stanco*), even if not overtly sexual. The conjunction of love and death in this context is not surprising: after all, the losing of oneself in orgastic passion has long been compared to a sort of death (*la petite mort*). In the end Death itself becomes the image of love, the consoling mother, the loving maiden on whose lap the poet lays his weary head: an archetypal erotic fantasy if ever there was one.

The conjunction of Eros and Thanatos occurs again in *Consalvo*, a romantic fantasy about the first and last kiss given by a woman to her dying lover, which Leopardi placed in the wrong chronological order in his 1835 edition of the *Canti*, as if it belonged to the 1821–3 period, but was in fact written about ten years later. 'Due cose belle ha il mondo/: amore e morte', [Two beautiful things has the world: love and death] says Consalvo. And Leopardi, in the second of his two letters to Fanny, of 16 August 1832:

> ... And yet certainly love and death are the only beautiful things the world has, and the only ones worth desiring. Think, if love makes man unhappy, what would the other things make him, which are neither beautiful nor worthy of man. (1, 1389, 2)

Love and death are also together in the page from Foscolo's *Ortis* describing the culmination of Jacopo's love for Teresa in a kiss (14 May 1798) which may be considered one of the sources of *Consalvo*. 'Oh for another kiss!' fantasizes Jacopo a few days later (27 May) 'and then leave me to my dreams and sweet wanderings of the mind; I shall die at your feet, wholly yours...'. Let us not forget that, in the chaste language of classicist poetry, a kiss is not only a kiss but also a metaphor for the sexual act to which it is often a prelude and which is invariably left unsaid. *Bacio* comes from the Latin BASIUM, a word introduced into Latin literature by Catullus, with the meaning of 'erotic kiss', distinct from that of OSCULUM which was a ritual kiss or a non-erotic display of affection between friends and relatives. The semantic change undergone by *baiser* in French is well-known. In the last poem that was inspired by his love for Fanny, *Aspasia*, Leopardi moves beyond metaphorical language and speaks quite plainly of *corporali amplessi* (bodily embraces, l. 45). That is the only time Leopardi uses the adjective *corporale* in the *Canti*. *Amplesso* occurs only once more, in *Alla Primavera* (l. 54), speaking of Daphne's body disappearing inside a laurel tree, which was, of course, one of the incarnations of her lover Apollo, who thus finally managed to possess her.

The point of these remarks is not only to dispel the image of a perennially virginal Leopardi, incapable of eroticism, and deprived throughout his life of the joys of sexual love, but also, and particularly, to give some factual reasons for the undeniably greater emotional depth of these love poems that were inspired by Fanny. Ranieri disliked them precisely because they were in his opinion *poesie erotiche*, and contrary to his image of a virgin Leopardi, the only sort of man a Neapolitan gentleman could have asked to live in the same house as his chaste sister. A reappraisal of the poems of the *Aspasia* cycle, which would not sweep their startlingly new erotic dimension under the carpet, might throw some new light on what actually happened between Leopardi and Fanny, who has been much reviled by biographers in their unnecessary efforts to protect Leopardi's virginity. Whether Leopardi had experienced sexual intercourse in Rome and Bologna or not, he remained for a long time unwilling to reconcile his sexuality (clearly acknowledged as early as 1819 in his letter to Xaverio Broglio d'Ajano; I, 1085, 1) with the emotion of love—a very common disability in people brought up in a strongly religious atmosphere.

> ... Sempre in quell'alma
> era del gran desio stato più forte
> un sovrano timor... (*Consalvo* ll. 19–21)
> [Always in that soul an overwhelming fear had been stronger than the great desire.]

Was it that 'overwhelming fear' that prompted the sudden flight of Leopardi to Rome in October 1831? In a letter to Carlo, Giacomo spoke of 'a long story, much sorrow, many tears' that perhaps he would tell him some day. He never did. Fear produced by love, and the psychological situation in which 'sexual intercourse ... does not even come into the mind' are described and analyzed with great subtlety in a note of 16 September 1823 in the *Zibaldone* (3443–6). That note was written in the present tense, whereas the lines of *Consalvo*, about ten years later are in the past, and describe a situation where that fear was at last overcome through a deep realization of the dialectical relationship between Eros and Thanatos, in other words, of the sexual nature of love. What exactly brought about that new awareness we shall never know in detail, but I would not exclude in principle the idea that, after Leopardi returned to Florence in March 1832, Fanny was

> … da pietà condotta
> a consolare il suo deserto stato (*Consalvo*, ll. 10, 11)
> [led by pity to console his desolate state.]

If that was indeed what happened, then the consequences of her friendly pity for Leopardi's infatuation were clearly and dispassionately set out in *Aspasia*, written when Leopardi could view his experience with a measure of detachment:

> … Vagheggia
> il piagato mortal quindi la figlia
> della sua mente, l'amorosa idea …
> … tutta al volto, ai costumi, alla favella
> pari alla donna che il rapito amante
> vagheggiare ed amar confuso estima.
> Or questa egli non già, ma quella, ancora
> nei corporali amplessi, inchina ed ama.
> Alfin l'errore e gli scambiati oggetti
> conoscendo s'adira; e spesso incolpa
> la donna a torto. … (ll. 37–48)
> [The wounded mortal therefore cherishes the creation of his own mind, the amorous idea…utterly similar, as to face, customs, way of speaking to the woman whom the enraptured lover believes, in his confusion, he loves and cherishes. In fact he does not worship and love the woman, even during sexual intercourse, but the idea. Eventually, recognizing his mistake and the exchange of love objects, he becomes angry, and often wrongly blames the woman.]

There is no trace of a break, as formerly with Teresa Malvezzi, in Leopardi's papers, nor in any known documents. Fanny is frequently mentioned in various letters to Ranieri between January and March 1833. On 29 January Giacomo informed Antonio that Carlino Torrigiani, the latest of Fanny's lovers, had left for New York, and that she had begun to show Leopardi great affection so that he would act as a go-between between her and Ranieri (1, 1397, 2). Then, after 21 March she simply disappears from Leopardi's epistolario, though she still kept inquiring after him in her letters to Ranieri, and remembered him dearly even after his death. His brother Carlo had vanished over a year earlier. Leopardi's last letter to Giordani was written in September 1832, commemorating a young man, 'the most happy Enrico' whom studying, drinking, smoking and wenching had brought to an enviable even if untimely end; and announcing his intention to leave for Naples (1, 1390). Giordani was rather bitter about what he called Leopardi's change 'from amorous frenzy to utter indifference'. The last mention of Puccinotti appears in the already quoted letter to Vieusseux of January 1832 (see p. 68 above), and Vieusseux was dropped after Leopardi's final departure from Florence in September 1833. I think Fanny, like the other devoted and steadfast friends of Leopardi, was simply the victim of a kind of retrenchment and withdrawal into himself, which Leopardi went through in that period, and to which he gave admirable and concise poetic expression in *A se stesso* [To himself], celebrating not so much his own despair—for that had been vented in many other poems—as the achievement of a final and complete self-awareness, the realization of the 'infinite emptiness of it all'. After the fulfilment of love the only thing that was left to Leopardi was the fulfilment of death. Aspasia, who once lived in his heart, now lay buried there (*Aspasia*, ll. 70–1, 77–9).

Almost to confirm the 'death' of Aspasia, Leopardi placed next in his 1835 edition of the *Canti* two funerary poems, *Sopra un bassorilievo antico sepolcrale dove una giovane morta è rappresentata in atto di partire accomiatandosi dai suoi* [On an Ancient Funerary Bas-Relief Where a Young Dead Woman is Portrayed as she takes Leave of her Family), and *Sopra il ritratto di una bella donna scolpito nel monumento sepolcrale della medesima* [On the Portrait of a Beautiful Woman Sculpted on her Funerary Monument], which I have reason to believe were written about the same time as *Amore e Morte* and not years later in Naples. They are both on the same theme expressed by Menander's aphorism Ὃν οἱ δεοὶ φιλοῦσιν ἀποθνήσκει νεός, 'He who is beloved by the Gods dies young', which Leopardi placed before that poem. They both contain echoes of the sea-image we have already examined in *Amore e Morte* (*Bassorilievo*, ll. 73–4; *Ritratto* ll. 39–49). But perhaps the most likely of all these conjectural reasons is that both poems were probably inspired by the illustrations accompanying Giuseppe Micali's great work *Storia degli antichi popoli italiani*, published in Florence in 1832. Leopardi knew the work to which his attention had been drawn both because its earlier edition was quoted in Niebuhr's *The History of Rome*, which he had been reading in 1828–9 (*Zib.*4431–2), and because it had received a prize from the Accademia della Crusca, and no doubt Leopardi had not neglected to find out about earlier recipients of that particular prize. Furthermore he had met Micali through Vieusseux in 1828 (I, 1336, 2), when the historian was busy recasting and enlarging his *L'Italia avanti il dominio dei Romani* (Florence 1810 and 1821), and the relative graphic documentation, *Monumenti inediti ad illustrazione della storia degli antichi popoli italiani*. Figure 60 of Micali's volume of illustrations represents what is now known as the Chiusi alabaster sarcophagus of Hasti, wife of Afuna, where a young dead woman, with the hand of Death resting gently on her shoulder, is portrayed as she takes leave of her family. The bas-relief, as Micali pointed out in his *Storia* (p. 100), represents in fact the parting between a wife and her husband. But, since the husband is portrayed as an older man and is accompanied by a mature woman, the bas-relief can easily suggest to the imagination that the dead woman is leaving not her husband's but her father's house (*il patrio tetto* l.4) and her parents (l.21) Another sarcophagus, with the portrait of a twenty-five-year old woman reproduced by Micali on page 105, fits the iconography of the second poem. The hypothesis that Micali's illustrations are the source of both poems is confirmed by the fact that in both of them the Death Angels appear as Etruscan *Lasae*, that is, unmistakably female. Not very much is known about the exact definition and meaning of this particular angel of death, and Micali was rather confused in dealing with that problem, in the context of a discussion of the dualistic principle allegedly present in the Etruscan religion. It is however interesting that in that discussion (vol. II, p.125) Micali remembered the Persian dualism of Ormuzd and Ahriman, for about that time Leopardi was thinking of writing a Hymn to that deity (see p.101). The Etruscan death angels, appearing so often as naked or scantily dressed girls in Micali's illustrations, may have inspired Leopardi to change the aspect of Death from the traditional winged youth with torch of the Graeco-Roman iconography, or from the repellent skeleton of mediaeval times, into a *bellissima fanciulla*.

12. The Relevance of Politics

No one becomes a man without going through a great test, which, by revealing himself to himself and shaping his opinion of himself, somehow determines his fortune and his condition in life...Most people die before having such an experience, so they are only slightly less childish than when they were born. To the others self-knowledge and self-possession come either from need and ill fortune or from some great—that is strong— passion; mostly from love, provided it is a great passion. This, unlike falling in love, does not happen to everybody. But once it has happened, whether early in life, as to some, or late, after other less important loves, as in most cases, it is certain that a man, after emerging from a strong and passionate love, has a pretty good knowledge of his fellow men, amongst whom he has had to endure his intense desires and pressing needs, not perhaps experienced previously. He is an expert in the nature of passions, since when one of them is inflamed it sets fire to all the others. He knows his own nature and temperament, and how far his faculties and strength can take him...Finally life, which has changed for him from hearsay into visible facts and from imagination into reality, takes on a new aspect and he feels he is in the thick of it, perhaps not happier than before but, so to speak, more powerful, in other words better able to make use of himself and others.

Unlike most of Leopardi's *Pensieri*, the eighty-second, which I have just quoted, has no source in the *Zibaldone*. It must therefore have been composed at the time when Leopardi was putting together and revising his collection of maxims and aphorisms, that is, between 1833 and 1837, probably in Naples. It reveals the results of his tempestuous and much discussed affair with Fanny Targioni-Tozzetti, and the new feeling of self-awareness and power he derived from the experience.

That Leopardi did not see love in isolation, but as an emotion capable of setting fire to all the others, is confirmed by *Il pensiero dominante*, cleary implying that other thoughts occupied the mind

where love was uppermost. Of them the one that is given most
space in the poem is Leopardi's polemical stance against the social
and political ideologies of the time:

> Sempre i codardi, e l'alme
> ingenerose, abbiette
> ebbi in dispregio. Or punge ogni atto indegno
> subito i sensi miei;
> move l'alma ogni esempio
> dell'umana viltà subito a sdegno.
> Di questa età superba,
> che di vote speranze si notrica,
> vaga di ciance, e di virtù nemica;
> stolta, che l'util chiede,
> e inutile la vita
> quindi più sempre divenir non vede;
> maggior mi sento.... (ll. 53–65)

[I always despised cowards, and ungenerous, abject minds.
Now every unworthy act stings my senses; every instance of
human dastardliness immediately moves my spirit to indignation. I feel above this boastful age, which feeds on empty
hopes, is fond of babble and is the enemy of virtue; this stupid
age, which sets utility as the highest requirement, and fails to
see that life becomes as a consequence more and more useless.]

Codardo is a word Leopardi used sparingly. Apart from this quotation
we find it only in the early *canzoni civili* (*Sopra il monumento di Dante*;
Ad Angelo Mai, twice; *Nelle nozze della sorella Paolina*) and in *Amore
e morte*, always in similar polemical contexts. The whole passage
resembles in tone the condemnation of *la vergognosa età* in *Nelle nozze
etc* (l.65) coming immediately after the statement that 'love spurs
one to lofty deeds'. There can be no doubt about its political significance. Of course, the connection between love and *egregi atti*, as
well as between the repression of sexual and erotic love and the
repression of any *egregi atti* tending towards social and political
change was obvious to anyone in the Romantic age who had read
Foscolo's *Ortis* and Goethe's *Werther*. It should be obvious today
for Wilhelm Reich, Herbert Marcuse and many others have illustra-
ted it. It was perfectly clear in Leopardi's mind, and it is difficult to
see why so many critics should have ignored it. The dates too speak
clearly. Leopardi wrote the three *canzoni civili* between 1820 and
1821, at the time, that is, of the revolutionary movements organized
by the *carbonari* in Naples, Milan and Turin. The time of his love for

Fanny was also the time of his friendship with Pietro Colletta, one of
the protagonists of the Neapolitan uprisings of 1820–1; and the
time of new revolutionary upheavals all over Europe (Paris, Belgium,
Switzerland, Poland) and in the very States of the Church of which
Count Giacomo Leopardi was a not-too-obedient subject. There the
uprising began in March 1831 in the *Legazioni* (Ferrara, Ravenna,
Bologna and Forlì) that had formed part of the Napoleonic Kingdom of Italy, and did not like the harsh and reactionary government
of the Cardinal Legates reimposed upon them after 1815. Soon the
various towns that had rejected the Pope's government began to
select suitable representatives to send to a Constituent Assembly in
Bologna. The town of Recanati chose as its deputy Giacomo Leopardi. By the time he received the nomination 4000 Austrian soldiers
had already marched through Florence on their way to Bologna and
Forlì, to quell the rebellion (1, 1356, 2). Leopardi could not therefore
accept his townspeople's mandate, and it is doubtful whether in those
circumstances he would have wanted to. The important point, however, is that he could not help being drawn into the political life of
those times. True, in the first of his two extant letters to Fanny he
declared that he abominated politics: it is nevertheless significant,
in the context of this connection between love and politics, that he
wrote to *her* about his political ideas. What did Leopardi mean when
he said he abominated politics? He certainly abominated Monaldo's
politics as expressed in the *Dialoghetti*, which Giacomo publicly and
bluntly repudiated in May 1832; apparently a sudden decision, since
he was very active in distributing, as late as April 1832 (1, 1380,
1), the very book he was to denounce the following month (1,
1380, 2; 1381–1383). 'Politics' for him had two meanings, ruling
class policies often supported by the ignorant, and the fact that man
is a social animal and should plan his existence accordingly. This is
shown by two pages of the *Zibaldone* written in November 1820.
In an age when everybody had a smattering of education, Leopardi
wrote, politics was cheapened by people of low intelligence who put
utopian schemes before 'sound and useful ideas'; which shows,
incidentally, that Leopardi was only against utilitarianism seen as the
worship of selfish profit (see also *Zib.*21–3). Politics, taken as the
enlightened science of 'the things that more closely, strongly and
universally concern us' was in Leopardi's opinion of paramount
importance:

> How can it be that, since politics is at all times relevant to his
> life, an unprejudiced man, used to thinking, should not make it

the principal object of his thoughts, and, as a consequence, of
his value judgements? [*gusto*]. (*Zib.* 310)

He believed that morality, though in theory more important, was in
practice subordinated to politics:

> Moral science is purely speculative, in so far as it is separated
> from politics. The life, the action and the practice of morality
> depend upon the nature of social institutions and the way a
> nation is governed: it is a dead science if politics does not co-
> operate with it and makes it reign over the nation. Speak of
> morality as much as you will to a badly ruled people—morality
> is words and politics is a fact. Family life, private social life, any
> human thing whatever, takes its shape from the general nature
> of the public state of a people. (*Zib.* 311)

His comments, in his letter to Fanny (I, 1369, 1) that the masses could
not be happy so long as they were made up of unhappy individuals,
show just as much concern for the happiness of the masses as for that
of the individuals; and great prescience, considering that the industrial revolution created large masses of unhappy exploited
workers under cover of bringing about their happiness.

After the failure of the 1820–1 uprisings Leopardi had thought of
using the weapon of satire to awaken his contemporaries to *egregi
atti*: out of those first satirical sketches came, as we know, the
Operette morali. After the failure of the new wave of uprisings ten
years later, he wrote his last two *operette: Dialogo d'un venditore
d'almanacchi e d'un passeggere* [Dialogue between an Almanach Seller
and a Passer-by] and *Dialogo di Tristano e di un amico* [Dialogue
between Tristan and a Friend]. The close connection between the
liberating emotion of love and the belief in ideals of freedom and
social concord is once more symbolized by the fact that the very last
operetta, containing a re-affirmation of Leopardi's anti-optimistic
ideology, contains also the quotation from Menander prefacing
Amore e morte, and the rejection of the false priority of the masses
over the individuals in nearly the same words as in his letter to Fanny.

This new awareness of himself and of real life, this new feeling of
self-possession and power which Leopardi derived from his last love
experience, was reflected not only in his sudden repudiation of his
father's book, but also in his renewed political commitment. In this
respect his last poetic works, *Paralipomeni della Batracomiomachia*
[A Continuation of the Battle between Frogs and Mice], *Palinodia
al Marchese Gino Capponi* [A Recantation, to Marquess Gino
Capponi], *I nuovi credenti* [The New Believers] and *La ginestra* [The

Broom] are similar to his first: only this time the depth and complexity of Leopardi's message was such that it could not be disguised and neutralized by critics as an imitation of classical models or an outburst of juvenile rhetoric. As a consequence all these poems have been neglected or condemned by the majority of commentators, with the exception of *La ginestra*, in which the beautiful descriptions of nature and the infinite universe, anticipating the 'cosmic poetry' of Tommaseo and Pascoli, have been judged so sublime as to redeem the more pedestrian philosophical and political passages.

To what extent can poetry be political? Though this is not the place for a general discussion of the question, we should take into account what Leopardi himself thought about that issue. In the quotation from *Zibaldone* 310 that I translated earlier, he said that politics should be the main object of a man's *gusto*, a word that implies also aesthetic value judgements, and therefore the criteria a poet uses in evaluating his own writings. The question reappears in the *Zibaldone* nearly three years later, in the context of a protracted analysis of the ideology of the epic poem and its national-popular function (pp. 3095–177), preparatory to the later discussion of popular epics which I mentioned in my comments on *Canto notturno* (p. 96–7). One of the problems that concerned Leopardi at that time was the historical conditioning of art, a question that would worry Karl Marx thirty-four years later, when he was writing his *Einleitung zur Kritik der politischen Oekonomie*: how is it that, in spite of the fact that Greek art presupposes Greek society and mythology, it is still a powerful source of inspiration today, when its society and mythology are dead? How is it, Leopardi asked, that Homer's poems are more alive than scores of other poetic works, equally subject to historical conditioning, like Tasso's *Gerusalemme liberata*, or even the *Aeneid*? He had already maintained in 1818 that they were incomparably more alive than Romantic poetry, paying lip service to the false myths of the ruling classes (see pp. 24–5 above). Leopardi's answer was that Greek poets followed only nature and themselves whereas later poets followed a series of restricting and misleading norms allegedly established by Greek poets. He nevertheless recognized the importance and the value of the political action of sixteenth-century writers and poets in promoting the cause of Christian unity against the Muslim menace (*Zib.* 3128–9), and the particular value of Tasso's work:

> who, in his poem, put religion and the opinions and the popular spirit of his time, and all other things that lend themselves to

poetry (granted that political speculation cannot be material for poetry) to the use of promoting the most important aim, which was then the preservation of civilisation, freedom, the political structure and the well-being of Europe as a whole... (*Zib.* 3175)

It should be noted that the propositions that 'political speculation cannot be material for poetry' and that poetry has a valuable political function are not contradictory. In other words, one should not versify political tracts, but what one writes can usefully express and support a political belief. Likewise, as we have already seen, Leopardi was of the opinion that philosophical propositions, scientific demonstrations, even sentimental effusions should not be the materials of poetry, which would then become a mere metrical paraphrase of pre-existing contents; but he would certainly not deny that poetry, immediately fashioned by the poet 'following nature and his own self' should be philosophical, put forward scientific truths and express emotions.

Leopardi translated and published three times the Greek poem *Batrachomyomachia* [The Battle of the Frogs and the Mice], of which he rejected the attribution to Homer. The first translation, done in 1815, appeared in the *Spettatore italiano e straniero* of Milan the following year. A revised version, written in 1821–2 was published in 1826 in *Caffé di Petronio* of Bologna. The final version to which Leopardi attended in 1826 was also published in Bologna that same year as part of the collection of Leopardi's *Versi* edited by Brighenti. It is not known when Leopardi thought of writing his 'continuation' of the *Batrachomyomachia* (the Greek title actually means 'what has been omitted from') but it must have been about 1832 given the references in the poem to the death of Niebuhr (2 January 1831) and the battle of Louvain (12 August 1831). The state of the manuscript, in Ranieri's hand, except the first canto which is an autograph, suggests that most of the poem was written in Naples. According to Ranieri it was finished shortly before the poet's death. Quite plainly the contents of the poem were inspired partly by the failure of liberal movements in Naples between 1820 and 1821, which Pietro Colletta had dealt with in his *Storia del reame di Napoli* [History of the Kingdom of Naples] the manuscript of which he wanted Leopardi to revise, and partly by the political situation of Italy after 1831. The ancient poem broke off soon after the unexplained intervention of the crabs, sent by Zeus to support the frogs, and the defeat of the mice. Leopardi's continuation explains this intervention according to

Metternich's theory of the European balance of power (II, 32–9). The hard crustaceans are the Austrians, 'police and executioners of Europe' (II, 37); the mice represent the Neapolitans, and in general any Italian state repressed by the Austrians for its aspirations to constitutional government; the frogs are those states the Austrians occupied and interfered with under the pretext of protecting them from the liberal menace. Leopardi's satire takes in all of them: in Ranieri's words, the poet's opinion was 'that the Austrians are a bunch of ignorant butchers, and the Italians a bunch of cowards'. Nor did Leopardi spare his irony against other targets, beginning with Vieusseux's Reading Room and its associates: Count Leccafondi seems to be a mixture of Vieusseux and Capponi (I, 34–43). He also satirized the racial prejudices and the confused idealism of some German scholars (I, 16–17), although he praised German culture where praise was due (III, 12–13; VIII, II, a reference to J.H.Voss and G.W.Nitzsch who proved that the belief in after-death retribution did not originate with Homer). He heaped scorn on the providential theory of history and the belief in the initial perfection of man (IV, 3–24); and on the belief in the immortality of the soul (VII, 18; VIII, 1–15). He defended his view that nature appears to us as an enemy, and that we should recognize that we cannot understand its ends, and perhaps that there are no such ends (IV, 12–13); and upheld the truth of the philosophy of the Enlightenment (IV, 16–17), which he would later praise in *La ginestra* (ll. 55–77).

The poem was written by Leopardi in the same *ottava rima* that Ariosto had used in *Orlando furioso*: a metre closely identified in the history of Italian literature with 'popular' poetry, that is, written not only for the *cognoscenti* but also for the people at large. It is at times remarkably funny and makes for very pleasant reading. It throws light on an aspect of Leopardi's mature character that those who stop at the *Canti* ignore at their peril. It represents a notable development on the irony of the *Operette morali* which never attained real humour, nor were meant to—a development that must in my opinion be related to the newly achieved self-awareness I attempted to define at the beginning of this chapter. About the time when Leopardi was attending to his last translation of the *Batracho-myomachia*, he noted in his *Zibaldone* that those who wish to succeed in satire or comedy must be themselves possible objects of satire and comedy (4173).While in Florence he had discovered 'the terrible and *awful* power of laughter' (the English word is in the original). 'He who is bold enough to laugh has mastery over the others, like the man who has the courage to die' (*Zib.*4391). Leopardi's awareness of the ridiculous aspects of his freely talked about involvement with Fanny was not apparently accompanied by the resentment he felt over Teresa Malvezzi's gossip. Perhaps by that time he had acquired the ability, theoretically perceived in Bologna, of laughing at himself. And the discovery of the power of laughter is in accord with his newly acquired feeling of power and mastery over himself and others which he mentioned in his eighty-second *Pensiero*.

The other two satirical poems, *I nuovi credenti* and *Palinodia*, are more likely to produce wry smiles than laughter. On *I nuovi credenti* it is difficult to better Benedetto Croce's commentary, projecting the poem on to the colourful background of Neapolitan life in the 1830s. That however was the only element in the poem he felt attracted by, since, unlike Leopardi, he believed that:

> the thoughts and theories on which Leopardi poured his scorn and irrision were the very thoughts and theories from which the movement of national resurgence began, actively and fruitfully, in Naples, and the men he insulted...co-operated in the re-awakening of studies and of the moral fervour of the citizens (*zelo civile*), by advocating the ideologies of liberal catholicism or neo-guelfism.

It is only fair to say that a number of serious and reputable historians would today agree more with Leopardi's than with Croce's judgement. It is doubtful whether the Risorgimento ever developed significantly in Naples to produce any real social change, or whether the ideologies advocated by those men increased in the least the happiness of individual Neapolitans. They, according to scores of later witnesses, including Francesco Mastriani, Renato Fucini and Matilde Serao, were still living, half a century after Leopardi's death, in conditions of unimaginable wretchedness and squalor. Vast numbers of them still are today. In *Palinodia*, written the year before, Leopardi reaffirmed his beliefs by pretending to recant them, as if he he had finally been won over to the ideas of Gino Capponi (who was a worthy conservative, very limited in outlook) by the irresistible march of progress. It is difficult to understand how this poem could have been the basis for a charge of political shortsightedness against its author, when the acumen and the farsightedness he displays in it are really amazing. The 'universal love' promised by the press (l.42) turned out to be a lie. The increase of commerce and trade did indeed produce bloodshed and strife (ll.43, 61–9), including a ruinous economic war in the United States of America (ll. 62–3) a quarter of a century after the poem was written. Leopardi clearly predicted the exploitation of the poor by the rich, which is the substance of colonialism and neo-colonialism (ll. 90–6). He foresaw consumerism (ll. 109–121 and 251–5) and the extraordinary power of mass-media (ll. 145–53). His strictures against statistics (ll. 137–45) would apply very well today to such sciences as econometrics and cliometrics where the counting up and measuring of phenomena seems to be an end in itself, rather than a means to arrive at sound economic, political and historical judgements.

What Capponi thought of this poem is known (see p. 67 above). One can only imagine what Tommaseo's reaction must have been in seeing himself pilloried (ll. 227–38). The opinion the Neapolitan government had of Count Giacomo Leopardi was no different from that of the Papal government, of the Florentine government, or of the Austrian government: the *Operette morali* published by Starita in 1836 were promptly seized and prohibited, together with the *Canti* published the year before. The only real pleasure Leopardi seems to have derived from his stay in Naples was the consumption of large quantities of sweetmeats, sorbets and ice-cream.

13. Light and Darkness

According to Croce the 'absurdity of Leopardi's didacticism and poetics' was that he wanted to 'disprove by means of ratiocinations on the worthlessness of life the happiness of those who actually felt happy'. This is of course a misrepresentation of Leopardi's attitude. We know he never tried to disprove Fanny's happiness, on the contrary he argued that her melancholy was 'rather unreasonable' (1, 1369, 1). He welcomed the happiness one feels after a threatening storm, or before a holiday. He would have liked to see people a lot happier than they were.

In his *Teoria del piacere* Leopardi was not so much concerned with ordinary day-to-day feelings of joy and sorrow as with establishing a general psychological-sociological theory of the human condition. In its simplest form, as can be deduced from *Zibaldone* 4186, the theory states that man 'naturally' yearns after absolute happiness, and since that is by definition unattainable, he is necessarily frustrated and unhappy. It follows that nature, which gives man such a yearning, is responsible for his unhappiness. Put that way, the argument has a seemingly inescapable logic, but there is, of course, a flaw. Leopardi was fully convinced that what man takes as absolutes are in fact culturally and socially conditioned opinions and misconceptions: so much so that he devoted many pages of the *Zibaldone* to replacing the belief in absolutes by moral, aesthetic and historical relativism, and to explaining why many forms of behaviour that appear to be absolutely innate in man are in fact due to culturally conditioned habits (*assuefazione*). It would have been an easy step for Leopardi to realize that man's yearning for happiness, whatever that means exactly, is not absolute or 'natural' in the sense that it is biologically inevitable, but culturally determined (he said in fact that people of lower intelligence do not exhibit it as much as sensitive cultured individuals). He could easily have ceased imputing man's unhappiness to nature, and pointed, as the real culprits, to those particular ideologies and philosophies that hold up unattainable ideals to man and try to convince him of his final salvation, ever increasing progress and wealth, ultimate happiness and similar empty and false mirages (and to a certain extent he did). It is very odd and disconcerting that Leopardi should go down in history as the arch-pessimist who believed in the fundamental and natural unhappiness of man; considering that those who passed as his optimistic and forward-looking opponents were Christians like Tommaseo, who believed in original sin and the inevitability of eternal damnation unless divine grace was mysteriously and gratuitously granted; the Risorgimento entrepreneurs who, by shaping society as a ladder, of which every private individual showing enough enterprise could allegedly reach the top, effectively turned life into a scramble where most people were doomed to lie trampled at the bottom; bourgeois liberals like Capponi, who believed in a well-ordered society in which the rich should help the poor, provided each class kept to its proper place ordained by God or Nature; not to speak of all those retrograde thinkers who believed in the 'naturalness' of many forms of human wretchedness and misery that were in fact caused by easily remediable social evils. They, and not Leopardi, were the real pessimists, the true champions of the inevitability of human unhappiness. They were the ones who 'would rather have darkness than light', in the words of the gospel of St John, which Leopardi placed before *La ginestra*.

If all this is true, it remains to be seen why, late in life, Leopardi changed his emphasis from the benevolent to the hostile aspect of nature; and why he ended by proclaiming that nature was the real cause of human misery and that man's unhappiness was inevitable: propositions demonstrably inconsistent, as we have seen, with his belief in the ethical neutrality of nature, and his theories of relativism and *assuefazione* (see pp. 70–1 and 80–1).

The final expression of the alleged hostility of nature, which crushes thousands of men in earthquakes and volcanic eruptions with the same heartless unconcern as she displays towards the inhabitants of an anthill destroyed by a falling apple, is to be found in *La ginestra o il fiore del deserto* [The Broom, or The Desert Flower] written at the foot of Vesuvius in 1836 (ll. 202–96). And yet Leopardi did not entirely obliterate the positive aspect of his ambivalent concept of nature, *dura nutrice* (l. 44) *madre di parto e di voler matrigna* (l. 125): she is hard and unfeeling but at the same time she is the one who gave us life and nourishes us. And nature's hostility is described in terms suggesting more passivity and indifference than active aggression. *La ginestra* contains also an attack on the duplicity and hypocrisy of all those who preferred the darkness of Restoration philosophies to the light of the Enlightenment (ll. 52–9) and wanted to enslave people's thought while paying lip-service to freedom (ll. 72–7); and of their followers, who flattered people's philosophical and political immaturity while despising them in their own hearts (ll. 59–63). Like the previous satirical poems, *La ginestra* also highlights the contradiction between the ideology of bourgeois progress and the amount of wretchedness it implied and actually generated. It is true that Leopardi presented this contradiction as if it was the contrast between a set of *ideas* on man's perfectibility and progress and the objective *fact* of man's puniness and irrelevance in the general scheme of nature. On the other hand there is no doubt, considering his criticism of human reason, that he knew it to be a contradiction internal to the ideology he rejected and had finally decided to attack, using the weapon of satire, once his prolonged contacts in Florence with political refugees and politically committed people, and the personal crisis described in the previous chapter, had sharpened his political consciousness.

It was not easy however to discredit the theories of those optimistic ideologists by showing only their *internal* contradictoriness. It would have been theoretically possible to deny the value of progressive and reformist beliefs, implying the notion of a providential order of things and the infinite perfectibility of man, by showing that those very beliefs, translated into policies of social control and economic exploitation of the lower orders (whose suffering was alleged to be for the common good), generated an untold amount of human wretchedness. But this idea, which is still very unpopular in certain quarters, would have been rejected out of hand in the 1830s, even if Leopardi could have managed the feat of producing a convincing demonstration. He had therefore to take the line that there was an inconsistency between the optimists' *ideas* and the independently established *fact* of human wretchedness. However, if human wretchedness had been attributed to moral corruption and sinfulness (as Manzoni later did in his *Remarks on Catholic Morals*), or (as Leopardi himself had done in his early *Zibaldone*) to man's deviation from an original perfect natural order, it would have been easy to show that there was no contrast, since progress, reforms, and faith in human perfectibility were the necessary foundations for any attempt to heal the acknowledged evils of the human condition—in due course the reformers' efforts would be crowned by success and the perfectly well-ordered society would come into being. Furthermore for Leopardi to say that unhappiness was inherent in man or caused inevitably by his faults, would have destroyed all basis for political thought and action (since, if that was true, nothing at all could be *done* about it), and contradicted Leopardi's own belief in relative progress and civilization. The only option open to him, therefore, was to say that the cause of man's inevitable unhappiness was outside man, and that the only remedy would be the formation of a chain of human solidarity, a brotherly union of all men in their struggle against nature, their common enemy (ll. 126–57). Thus he indirectly attacked the social divisiveness and exploitation that was one of the prime consequences of bourgeois progress.

Nature stands majestic, aloof in *La ginestra*, as in the *Dialogo della Natura e di un islandese*. She is the enemy, but an enemy that does not so much inspire fear as awe and respect. To fight against such an enemy can only enhance man's nobility and spiritual stature (ll. 111–25): therein lies real civilization and progress. For a man to believe in his own omnipotence is a sign of immaturity and childishness (*pargoleggiar*, l. 59) that paradoxically goes together with lack of freedom and with utter dependence: a child, as psychologists tell us, feels omnipotent only insofar as his every need is satisfied by his mother. To realize the dangers of this dependence and ultimately to break its bond is the task of maturity, which brings about a clear awareness of one's own limitations, and the stimulus to overcome them. The personal history of Leopardi the man was the constant and relentless overcoming of his own innate and acquired disabilities. There is perhaps some justification for the widespread critical opinion that *La ginestra* is made up of lyrical passages and philosophical parts of unequal poetic value. Its unusual formal and conceptual richness and its length (it is the longest of the *Canti*) make it difficult to grasp its fundamental artistic unity. Much time and space could be spent in illustrating its subtle metrical patterns, its irregular but melodious correspondences of rhymes and assonances, its arresting images. Lyrical passages and philosophical arguments must be seen in the context of a dialectical structure based on the idea of contrast, and of the rejection of any form of compromise tending to minimize contrast, which is reflected in the formal arrangement. The initial opposition between the slender grace of the flower and the arid and threatening ruggedness of the volcano is echoed throughout the poem by a constant interplay between harsh and harmonious images, like the description of the ants' 'sweet homes' dug out of the soft soil, and the pitiless natural cataclysm that destroys men's homes as if they were part of an ant-hill; or the description of the deadly lava flow twice juxtaposed to more serene visions of sea landscapes to which the word *flutto* would be conventionally considered more appropriate. Contrast is present both in the conceptual opposition between large structures (e.g. stanzas 2 and 3 expressing diametrically opposed views of man's dignity and stature in the universe) and in the presentation side by side of antithetical words, such as *dura nutrice* [harsh nurse] or *flutto indurato* [hardened flow]. Leopardi underlines his poetic discourse by constant references to earlier *Canti*. One is reminded, in reading *La ginestra* of the desolate landscapes seen in *A un vincitore nel gioco del pallone* and *Bruto minore* suggesting an atmosphere of eschatological ruin and destruction (ll. 14–23); of the poet's heroic opposition to his own times (ll. 64 and 305) heralded in *All'Italia* and confirmed in *Amore e Morte*; of the cosmic feeling which at the same time unites man with the universe, makes him reflect on his own insignificance and, through the awareness of his precarious position in nature, gives him an essential insight into his own dignity (ll. 157–201), so poignantly expressed in *Canto notturno*.

La ginestra can be taken as Leopardi's spiritual testament. This is perhaps why it was placed by Ranieri at the end of his 1845 edition of the *Canti*. Actually the last poem Leopardi wrote was *Il tramonto della luna* [The Setting of the Moon], possibly completed only a few hours before his death. It is a short and moving compendium of Leopardian themes, represented by typical words calling back to one's memory their earlier contexts (*solinga, campagne, infinito, scolora, il carrettier, l'età mortale, la giovinezza, i dilettosi inganni, morte, mali, vecchiezza, desìo, speme, piacer, piagge, luce, vedova, notte, sepoltura*). The poem conjures up an atmosphere of peaceful but final and all-pervading darkness. No more ambiguities, no more contrasts of light and shade, no more confused and deceptive images in the distance, no more illusions:

> giunta al confin del cielo
> dietro Apennino od alpe, o del Tirreno
> nell' infinito seno
> scende la luna; e si scolora il mondo;
> spariscon l'ombre, ed una
> oscurità la valle e il monte imbruna.

> [having reached the boundary of the sky, the moon sets behind the Apennines or the Alps, or in the infinite bosom of the Tyrrhenian sea; and the world fades away, the shadows disappear, and one and the same darkness blackens valleys and hills.]

The last word of the poem, and of Leopardi as a poet, is *sepoltura*, the grave. A few hours after having dictated it to Ranieri (according to a friend of his and of Bunsen's, the German poet Wilhelm Heinrich Schultz), Leopardi, who was by then suffering from dropsy, had difficulty in breathing. This was not very unusual. He had been very ill for some time. Ranieri and his sister Paolina had been assisting him to the best of their ability, in spite of their difficult financial circumstances, often depending on whatever money Giacomo managed to borrow from his friends or wheedle out of his mother's tight purse. But all their undoubted devotion, and all the care of the Neapolitan doctors could do very little for a man whose continual physical and psychological suffering had by then undermined his very will to live. It was not easy to find a doctor: Naples was in the grip of a cholera epidemic. Antonio went out personally to look for Dr Mannella. When they came back Leopardi was in better spirits, but Mannella at once advised Ranieri to send for a priest. Leopardi began to sweat profusely while Paolina was holding his head; then looking fixedly at Antonio, with eyes wide open, he whispered: 'I cannot see you any more'. It was about six o'clock in the afternoon of 14 June 1837. When the priest arrived Leopardi was already dead. The moon had set forever. Eternal night had finally overcome the most enlightened mind of his generation. The long and painstaking process of obscuring the revolutionary contents of Leopardi's thought, of denying the philosophical validity of his speculation, of reducing him to the status of a mere lyrical poet (even if the greatest lyrical poet of the age), of misrepresenting his convictions, was about to begin. In spite of the brave isolated efforts of some critics who, already in the second half of the last century, had recognized the significance of Leopardi's anti-optimistic message, its neutralization was to continue for over a century after his death. It was only in comparatively recent times that a different and truer picture of Leopardi began to emerge. I hope that this study may have sharpened some details of the picture, and that my portrait of a man and a poet I love may attract to Leopardi some more among the 'young men of the twentieth century', to whom he would have liked to write a letter when he was himself a young man; so that they too may experience the truth of Filippo Ottonieri's aphorism — 'Reading is a conversation one has with the writer', and enjoy the pleasure of conversing with a writer who 'said many good and beautiful things and said them very well' (I, 138–9).

CHAPTER ONE: 'Dearest Father ...'
The quotations from Leopardi's early works are from *Entro dipinta gabbia*, ed.
by MARIA CORTI (Milan 1972) 417, 154, 161; see also the preface, xxi
and xxvii. The biographical details are taken from M. L. PATRIZI *Saggio
psicoantropologico su G. L.* (Turin 1896) 64, 66; E. COSTA *Lettere di P.
Leopardi a M. e A. Brighenti* (Parma 1887) 8; M. LEOPARDI *Autobiografia*
(Milan 1971) 73; G. CUGNONI *Opere inedite di G. L. pubblicate sugli auto-
grafi recanatesi*, vol. I (Halle 1878) lvi–lx; G. LEOPARDI *Epistolario*, ed. by
F. MORONCINI and others (Florence 1934–41) vol. I, 198–200; D.
MANETTI *G. L. e la sua famiglia* (Milan 1950) 58, 86; C. ANTONA-
TRAVERSI *I genitori di G. L.*, (Recanati 1887–91) vol. I, 17–18, 280–1, 285–6.
Alphonse Daudet's opinion is in the broadsheet *A G. L.*, by various
authors (Città di Castello 1887) 3, quoted by H. HAHL, *Les tendances
morales dans l'œuvre de G. L.* (Helsingfors 1896). See also the biographies by
G. FERRETTI *Vita di G. L.* (Bologna 1940); IRIS ORIGO, *Leopardi, A
Biography* (Oxford U.P. 1935); I. DE FEO, *Leopardi: l'uomo e l'opera* (Verona
1972).

CHAPTER TWO: 'Peregrine and Recondite Erudition'
J. H. WHITFIELD's words are taken from his *G. L.* (Oxford 1954) 26. On
Pietro Giordani see S. TIMPANARO's introduction to the 1961 re-print of
P. GIORDANI, *Scritti*, ed. by G. CHIARINI (Florence 1890); and also his
Classicismo e illuminismo nell' Ottocento italiano (Pisa 1969) (2 ed.), a funda-
mental text for the study of Leopardi.

CHAPTER THREE: From Erudition to Poetry
The impact of Foscolo's *Ortis* and Goethe's *Werther* on Leopardi's poetry
is discussed in a most interesting and stimulating book by G. MANACORDA,
Materialismo e Masochismo: il 'Werther', Foscolo e Leopardi (Florence 1973)
referred to also in the following chapter.

CHAPTER FOUR: From Poetry to Philosophy
Gioberti's letter is in V. GIOBERTI, *Ricordi biografici e carteggio*, ed. G. MASSARI
(Naples 1868) vol. IV, 56; quoted by NOVELLA CELLI-BELLUCCI, 'V.G.
di fronte alla ideologia e alla poesia di L.', *Rassegna storica della letteratura
italiana* 78 (1974) 119. On the relationship between Gioberti and Leopardi
see also G. DE LIGUORI, 'V.G. e la filosofia leopardiana', *Problemi* 28,
1178–85. On Leopardi and Mme de Staël see SOFIA RAVASI, *L. et Mme de
Staël* (Milan 1910). The quotations of Mme de Staël are taken from *Oeuvres
complètes* (Paris 1820) vol. III, 245, 253, 254; and vol. XI, 311–15.

CHAPTER FIVE: 'Investigation of Relationships'
On *il sonetto negato* see ANNA DOLFI *L. tra negazione e utopia* (Padua 1973).
The whole question of the possible connection between Luis de Leon and
Leopardi has been discussed by A. MARTINENGO, 'La Spagna e lo spagnuolo
di L.', *Lettere Italiane* 24 (1972), n.2, 145–65, where references to previous
studies by ORTIZ, TORRACA and MATARRESE can be found. Very interesting notes on the nirvanic image of the sea can be read in A. EHRENZWEIG
The Hidden Order of Art, (St Albans 1973) 15, 95, 136 (the whole book is a
very rich source of ideas for the student of literature). More on *vago* and

indefinito in C. GALIMBERTI's valuable book *Linguaggio del vero in L.* (Florence 1959).

CHAPTER SIX: The 'Civic Odes' and Other Poems
The double life of Brighenti was revealed by G. CARDUCCI 'Le tre canzoni patriottiche di G. L.' now in *Opere: Edizione Nazionale*, vol. XX (Bologna 1937). See also G. BERTONI, 'Un candido amico del L.: Pietro Brighenti' in *Giornale Storico della Lett. Ital.* 56 (1936) nn. 322–3, pp. 80–6. For more information on the relationship between L. and Mai, turn to S. TIMPANARO *La filologia di G. L.* (Florence 1955). On the political reasons for the banning of *Ad Angelo Mai* see G. CARDUCCI op. cit.. P. BORSIERI's epigram is in E. BELLORINI, ed., *Discussioni e polemiche sul Romanticismo (1816–1826)* (Bari 1943) vol. I, 102–3.

CHAPTER SEVEN: 'A Touch of Irony'
On L.'s supposed Platonism see the valuable article by V. DI BENEDETTO 'G.L. e i filosofi antichi', in *Critica storica* VI (1967) 289–320.

CHAPTER EIGHT: Pessimism or Anti-optimism
On the Florentine circles in which L. moved see R. CIAMPINI, *G. P. Vieusseux, I suoi viaggi, i suoi giornali, i suoi amici* (Turin 1953) and U. CARPI, *Letteratura e società nella Toscana del Risorgimento* (Bari 1974); together with TIMPANARO's comments in 'Belfagor' 1975: 129–56, 395–428; 1976: 1–32, 159–200. Manzoni's low opinion of L. was quoted by M. MANDALARI *In memoria di F. De Sanctis* (Naples 1884) 117–18. Montani's portrait of the Romantic intellectual was reproduced by A. BORLENGHI, *La polemica sul Romanticismo* (Padua 1968) 277–8. Capponi's insulting reference to L. can be read in *Lettere di Gino Capponi e altri a lui*, (Florence 1882) vol. I, 404; the police's report on L. in FERRETTI's biography, 309–10. Francesco Puccinotti mentioned his conversation with L. about Ruysch in a curious autobiographical page in which he recounted how Leopardi learned English, by memorizing verbs and grammatical rules while waiting for the ink on each page of his manuscript to dry (DEFEO, *G.L.* cit., 71). I have dealt in greater detail with the question of L.'s scientific culture in a paper, *L. e la scienza* presented at the IX Congresso dell' Associazione Internazionale per gli Studi di lingua e letteratura italiana in April 1976, which is about to be published in the conference proceedings. On the scientific nature of the question of pleasure and pain, see S. TIMPANARO, *Sul materialismo* (Pisa 1970) 48.

CHAPTER NINE: 'The Soul of Everything is Contrast'
DE LOLLIS's essay has now been reprinted in *Scrittori d'Italia* (Milan-Naples 1969). LEACH's words on the binary process of human thought are from *Genesis as Myth and other essays* (London 1969) 9. The question of L.'s shift between two conceptions of nature has been discussed by S. TIMPANARO in *Classicismo e illuminismo* cit., 395 seq. where earlier articles by BIRAL, SOLMI and others are referred to. I will however venture a new hypothesis in the final chapter of this book.

CHAPTER TEN: Memory and Memories
Teresa Lucignani's memories have been brought to the attention of Leopardian scholars by R. WIS, *G.L.: studio biografico* (Helsinki 1959) 106–11.

Leopardi's two anthologies have been recently republished, with two illuminating prefaces by their editors: G. BOLLATI, *Crestomazia italiana: la prosa*, and G. SAVOCA, *Crestomazia italiana: la poesia*, both Turin 1968. The date of *Il passero solitario* has been discussed among others by A. MONTEVERDI, *Frammenti critici leopardiani* (Naples 1967) (2nd ed.); MARIA CORTI, 'Passero solitario in Arcadia' in *Metodi e fantasmi* (Milan 1969); D. DE ROBERTIS 'La data dei canti' (Postilla I) in *Leopardi e l'Ottocento: Atti del II Convegno Internaz. di studi leopardiani* (Florence 1970); and G. GETTO *Studi leopardiani* (Florence 1966) containing also references to the sources. Pascoli's criticism of *Il sabato del villaggio* is in 'Pensieri e discorsi', now in *Prose* (Milan 1947). The two existing concordances of Leopardi are by ANTONIETTA BUFANO, *Concordanze dei 'Canti' del L.* (Florence 1969) (limited to the *Canti*) and by L. LOVERA and CHIARA COLLI in G. LEOPARDI, *Canti, Paralipomeni, poesie varie, traduzioni poetiche e versi puerili*, ed. by C. MUSCETTA and G. SAVOCA (Turin 1968) (including all the works mentioned in the title, except the *puerili*).

CHAPTER ELEVEN: Love and Death
On the relationship between L. and Fanny Targioni-Tozzetti see U. BOSCO 'Un' ipotesi su Aspasia' in *Titanismo e pietà in G. L.* (Florence 1957). A. RANIERI's *Sette anni di sodalizio con G.L.* has been republished with an introduction by V. RUSSO (Naples 1965). G. BATAILLE's essay can be read in *L'érotisme* (Paris 1957) (ch. IV).

CHAPTER TWELVE: The Relevance of Politics
A very convincing account of the genesis of L.'s satirical poem is G. SAVARESE's *Saggio sui Paralipomeni di G.L.* (Florence 1967). B. CROCE's comment to *I nuovi credenti* is in his *Aneddoti di varia letteratura* (Naples 1942) vol. III, 102–13.

CHAPTER THIRTEEN: Light and Darkness
The revolutionary implications of L.'s thought had been perceived not only by various Italian police censors but also by several nineteenth-century critics; among whom Carducci, who thought that L.'s '*si accostava al socialismo*' (came near to Socialism, in 'Degli spiriti e delle forme nella poesia di G.L.', *Opere—Ediz.Naz.* vol. XX (1944/94); an opinion accepted and confirmed by G. ROMANO-CATANIA, *D'un nuovo libro scientifico sopra G.L.* (Palermo 1899) 41, who also quoted similar ideas expressed by G. MARTINOZZI during a lecture held in Bologna, (*Per la continuità nella vita nazionale,* Bologna 1897) and by F. MOMIGLIANO soon afterwards in his *Pessimismo e socialismo* (which I have not been able to see). To view L. as a socialist is, of course, a crude simplification, but it would be wrong to dismiss it out of hand, since it is the first symptom of a 'progressive' interpretation of L.'s work that has gained wider acceptance after the publication of C. LUPORINI's 'L. progressivo' in *Filosofi vecchi e nuovi* (Florence 1947) preceded by a selection of anarchist and revolutionary thoughts culled from the pages of the *Zibaldone* (G.L. *Pensieri anarchici,* ed. F. BIONDOLILLO, Rome 1945) and followed by W. BINNI's *La nuova poetica leopardiana,* (Florence 1947). Later S. TIMPANARO reviewed the whole question in *Classicismo e illuminismo*, cit., 133–7. Quite independently

(judging from the bibliography appended to his *G.L.*) J. H. Whitfield stressed in 1954 the active, positive, constructive side of L.'s uncompromising rejection of false optimism. I find his 'no obscurantism, no backsliding' more convincing as a motivation for L.'s anti-optimistic stance than Bosco's concept of *titanismo*. Romantic 'titanism' *à la* Alfieri was the forerunner of the decadent love for the 'superman': both were the exasperation of an individualistic love for freedom dangerously leaning towards antisocial or asocial consequences. Leopardi's attitude was never antisocial, and (if Titans must be mentioned) could better be called 'Prometheism'.